OTABIN

D0330363

Dear Friend:

You may have noticed that this book is put together differently than most other quality paperbacks. The page you are reading, for instance, along with the back page, is glued to the cover. And when you open the book the spine "floats" in back of the pages. But there's nothing wrong with your book. These features allow us to produce what is known as a detached cover, specifically designed to prevent the spine from cracking even after repeated use. A state-of-the-art binding technology known as OtaBind® is used in the manufacturing of this and all Health Communications, Inc. books.

HCI has invested in equipment and resources that ensure the books we produce are of the highest quality, yet remain affordable. At our Deerfield Beach headquarters, our editorial and art departments are just a few steps from our pressroom, bindery and shipping facilities. This internal production enables us to pay special attention to the needs of our readers when we create our books.

Our titles are written to help you improve the quality of your life. You may find yourself referring to this book repeatedly, and you may want to share it with family and friends who can also benefit from the information it contains. For these reasons, our books have to be durable and, more importantly, user-friendly.

OtaBind® gives us these qualities. Along with a crease-free spine, the book you have in your hands has some other characteristics you may not be aware of:

• Open the book to any page and it will lay flat, so you'll never have to worry about losing your place.

• You can bend the book over backwards without damage, allowing you to hold it with one hand.

• The spine is 3-5 times stronger than conventional perfect binding, preventing damage even with rough handling.

This all adds up to a better product for our readers—one that will last for years to come. We stand behind the quality of our books and guarantee that, if you're not completely satisfied, we'll replace the book or refund your money within 30 days of purchase. If you have any questions about this guarantee or our bookbinding process, please feel free to contact our customer service department at 1-800-851-9100.

We hope you enjoy the quality of this book, and find understanding, insight and direction for your life in the information it provides.

**Health Communications, Inc.®**

3201 S.W. 15th Street
Deerfield Beach, FL 33442-8190
(305) 360-0909

Peter Vegso
President

# CHRONICALLY
# SINGLE WOMEN

# CHRONICALLY SINGLE WOMEN

## How To Get Out Of The Singles Trap

KAREN JENKINS, M.S.W.

**Health Communications, Inc.**
**Deerfield Beach, Florida**

**Library of Congress Cataloging-in-Publication Data**

Jenkins, Karen
    Chronically single women : how to get out of the singles trap /
Karen Jenkins.
      p.    cm.
    Includes bibliographical references.
    ISBN 1-55874-299-9 (pbk.) : $9.95
    1. Single women — Psychology.   2. Mate selection.  I. Title.
HQ800.2.J45   1994                               94-3965
646.7'7—dc20                                    CIP

Publisher: Health Communications, Inc.
            3201 S.W. 15th Street
            Deerfield Beach, Florida 33442-8190

*Cover design by Barbara Bergman*
*Cover photo by Robert Fein*

*To the*
*many women*
*who are alone not*
*by choice:*

*May this book*
*illuminate the road*
*you travel and help*
*you find the relationship*
*you desire and*
*deserve.*

# ❀ Acknowledgments

*T*he road leading to the publication of this book has been illuminated by a number of individuals, and I would like to acknowledge each of them for their contribution to the process. First of all, I would like to thank my husband, Paul, for his willingness to share with me the journey of married life, for encouraging me to pursue my dreams, and for tutoring me in the use of the computer. I am also grateful to his friend, and my new friend, Jeff Andrus of The Writing Company, for his early encouragement and consultation. I am especially grateful to the many patients and workshop participants who have shared their experience with me, and helped me to see the many faces of the chronically single woman. And finally, my thanks to Barbara Nichols at HCI for the steady stream of support for this project.

As a former chronically single woman myself, I also want to acknowledge some of the individuals who hastened my own recovery. Many friends, mentors and helpers have encouraged me in the relationship which would become my marriage; for their support, I will be eternally grateful. These include my dearest friends, Lennette and Paula, who listened to all of my reasons for wanting to bail out, and just kept smiling and nodding; Maureen, whose own marriage reminded me of the possibilities; my priest, Fr. Rob, who helped me let love in; and Selma, who empowered me to be fully me. Thanks to all.

# ❀ *Contents*

# ❀ *Preface*

*T*here is nothing inherently wrong with single life. For those who freely choose it, it can be a rich, fulfilling experience. Throughout history there have been men and women who reveled in single life or who only accomplished what they did because they were alone, unfettered by the demands of a committed intimate relationship.

For many women, however, being single is not a chosen lifestyle, but a deeply painful and disappointing, and perhaps confusing, experience. Some have suffered through a social drought so severe they feel they will dry up and blow away. Some have had several dysfunctional relationships, perhaps including marriage and divorce. "Why am I still alone?" they ask — and well-intentioned friends remind them that women are marrying later these days.

That is indeed true. Many women today are exercising some of the freedoms denied their foremothers: they are electing to spend more time coming to know themselves in the world before choosing a mate — to work or to study, or even to play, before settling down. Many women today also enjoy much greater self-esteem than did their foremothers: they are turning down proposals their grandmothers might have felt obliged, or even pleased, to accept. Given more opportunities to earn their own way and greater understanding of their own needs, along with greater respect for them, women are paying less attention to a man's financial security and more to his emotional availability. Today we want a man who can talk to us, share his feelings, and hear and respond to ours. And, of course, we want a good lover.

It is tempting for the woman who finds herself persistently or repeatedly alone to blame men for her difficulties in getting close to them. In mainstream American culture men have not been trained to share their feelings or power, but to provide financial security and hold authority. Many hold it too tight. Over the past twenty years, however, the great changes in our culture have affected not only women but also men. The recovery movement has grown substantially, sensitizing men as well as women to the significance of childhood experiences and the need to grow beyond childhood losses. Twelve-step programs have grown like wildfire, teaching participants the healing power of accountability and offering tools to help address unmet needs. And the men's movement is helpful for men who wish to explore what it means to be male and emotional, and to seek a new definition of male power, without domination. The result is that growing numbers of men and women are discarding old sex role stereotypes, which really served no one's deepest needs, and are exploring a new form of coupling — partnership.

It is also tempting for the woman who is alone to blame her plight on circumstance: not enough good men. The fact is that there are more single men than single women in the twenty- and early thirty-year-old age group; so women in that group must look to themselves for the reason they are single. Even single women born before 1955, now outnumbering single men of the same era because of the war in Vietnam, are beginning to realize that *they* may be the real cause of their singleness.

When I began developing programs for chronically single women some ten years ago, I expected to see women over thirty who had never been married; I had no idea that so many women, in so many circumstances, would identify with the concept. The youngest woman, in her early twenties, said she saw the writing on the wall: she attracted little attention from men despite her pleasing appearance and sweet temperament; she had suffered from a painful shyness since her childhood, in reaction to an alcoholic father's violent outbursts. The oldest woman was in her early sixties: she had been abandoned by her husband many years before and had hidden behind her bitterness until a daughter's divorce and remarriage put her in touch with her pain and her wish for companionship.

Each of these women identified herself as "a chronically single woman" — a woman who at least thinks she wants to be in a committed, intimate relationship but finds herself persistently or repeatedly alone, or involved in relationships that cannot progress into commitment. They came for help, as have more than a hundred others, not knowing what was wrong but knowing intuitively that they were defeating themselves — either by distancing themselves from men altogether or by binding themselves to a man, or to one man after another, who could not become a lifelong mate. Their recovery began when they became aware of their own self-defeating behaviors, and it led them to practice new ways of relating to men, while dealing with the unconscious conflicts behind the self-sabotage.

This book is intended as a guide for chronically single women — to help you to develop awareness of the many subtle, and not so subtle, varieties of self-defeating behavior that may be at work in your relational patterns. It invites you to examine your behavior, not because you are to blame, but because you are the only person you can change. It draws on my experience in treating these women, and interviewing many more, as well as on my own experience as a woman marrying for the first time at the age of thirty-seven. It draws on the experience of these women, their problems and their recovery — real women, whose names have been changed, along with occasional details, to protect their privacy. Most of these women are heterosexual and unmarried; but their stories are wide ranging in terms of sexual orientation, marital status, and life circumstance. It is hoped they will help clarify your problem and lead you to recovery, to a happy relationship.

# Part One

# SELF-DEFEATING BEHAVIOR

# 1

# *Fear, Shame And Inhibition*

Do you remember how you felt as you prepared for your first date? Excited? On top of the world? And a bit anxious — even fearful? Most of us are apprehensive when we embark on new experiences and feel somewhat self-protective and self-conscious. For most, these uncomfortable feelings fade as the new experience becomes familiar. But for some women, uncomfortable feelings about dating don't fade and, in fact, become more intense as time goes on.

In the process of courting and dating we reveal to another who we are. That's what it's about — the self-revelation essential to finding a suitable mate. We have to be willing to be known — at first by our appearance and behavior; next by our opinions and values and our strengths and weaknesses; and ultimately by our souls.

When women are afraid to be known, the fear is likely to stem from poor self-esteem. Not feeling very good about yourself makes it difficult to let others get close. Perhaps someone has judged you harshly — a family member or someone you thought was a friend. And you fear a harsh judgement again.

You may feel insecure about your appearance, your body or your clothing. It's not unusual to feel concerned about your looks in a society that tells us that we need to conform to its standards to make ourselves attractive. A woman who has a sense of self-worth can manage to keep her perspective about her appearance.

For some women the self-esteem problem goes much deeper than "looks." More than not feeling good about how we look, or what we have, it involves not feeling good about who we are. It often stems from some real or imagined mistake in life — from something we have done or failed to do for which we have not forgiven ourselves. It could also stem from unjust blame we have bought into. Sometimes it is a mystery: we feel inferior and we don't know why.

This self-esteem problem is called shame, and it can be crippling to a woman's social life. Shame inhibits her willingness to be known. Most disastrously, it can make a woman want to hide — and true love seldom finds its way into hiding places. Some hide behind workaholism, some behind public service. Some hide behind a mask, choosing to be seen as a social butterfly or a clown or perhaps a cynic. These defenses may not be enough when a woman's shame is severe; she may withdraw from social relationships and remain a prisoner in her own shame.

Some women are not so much ashamed of who they are, as they are unsure. Such a woman fails to express herself because she does not know what to express. This lack of self-knowledge can also be crippling to her social life. Such a woman does not attract many men — not because they dislike her, but because they can't see her. She can't see herself. When she does attract men, it may be too frightening for her. It feels risky to let someone get close when you don't know who you are, and it is risky because identity is a frame of reference against which we evaluate our world. How can you trust your instincts about others when you have no frame of reference? How can you choose a mate without a real sense of who you are?

The struggle to define oneself is ideally resolved by young adulthood, but many things can prolong the struggle. Some families just don't want to let go and fail to encourage individuation. Perhaps a mother needs a mirror image of herself to admire to make herself feel better, or a companion to stave off loneliness. Or a father may enforce his strong opinion about what a young women should do with her life, not allowing her to develop on her own. Often a young woman is driven to fulfill the unfulfilled dreams of a parent.

Even when the parents are able to let go and support their daughter in finding her own self, other life traumas may leave her reluctant to look inside. She may be unwilling to let go of her parents, preferring to hang onto the safety of childhood. So she stays stuck in a comfortable, but perilous, trap — rewarded to some extent by a society that looks fondly upon the selfless devoted daughter.

Whatever the cause, when a woman's identity is poorly defined, a void is created. Some women cope with the inner void by borrowing identity from others, or perhaps by behaving in a way that will be pleasing to others. Identity may be borrowed from parents, peers, or boyfriends, or from anyone whose approval the woman is seeking. The borrowing is often easy, and positive as well, when it matches part of the borrower's true identity; still the identity has not been owned, and she feels shame as a sort of impostor.

Not all women with identity problems borrow identity to fill the void; some quietly tolerate it, hoping perhaps that the "mystery" of who they are will attract someone. When it does, these women are apt to be fearful of being exposed as empty shells, or fearful of being dominated, as can easily happen.

Many women express a desire to know themselves better. Often they have been searching for themselves for quite a while. When they stop looking outside for identity and begin to look inside, they are often frightened to find nothing. Some speak of "the black hole" as a vacuum, and some feel as if something is missing or as if something has been taken from them. Some fear that a horrible secret is hidden in there. The initial encounter with this sense of emptiness is usually terrifying — and unfortunately, their fears may turn out to be grounded in reality. Many women actually do have experiences that make it terrifying to really be themselves.

For others, the emptiness feels like a fertile void. They identify with being a vessel, or an incubator for creation. These women find peace, as well as a sense of their power as women, in identifying with their creative inner space.

When a woman is uncertain about who she is, she will instinctively defend herself by avoiding real contact with others. Although her conscious desire may be to share life with someone special, her unconscious need may be to remain alone. Typically, despite her professed desire to find a mate, she will behave in ways that defeat her ostensible purpose — and keep suitable mates at bay.

One very effective way to keep men away is to avoid eye contact. This is a natural defense if we wish not to be known, for eyes are the windows to the soul: they can give us away when we are denying hurt feelings, anger or need. On the other hand, eye contact is a handy tool when we want to communicate a simple message — that we are ready to leave a boring party, for instance. And eye contact is a powerful tool when we want to communicate interest, or desire. When we are sincere about seeking attention from men, and ready for it, we look men in the eye. And if we like what we see, we keep looking. So do they. The simple gaze is one of the most powerful forms of flirtation.

For the woman who is overly inhibited, however, sustained eye contact is nearly impossible. As eye contact is sustained, men seem to look right into you. Are you ashamed of the you they will see? Do you cast down your eyes?

> This was the third singles party Melanie had attended that year, and it was only February. As she approached the building where the party was in progress, Melanie heard the loud music and the dull roar of conversation. She remembered all the singles parties she had attended. She wondered whether this party would be different for her. Everyone else always seemed to know how to make conversation, how to meet the guys, to make friends. Not Melanie — she was never at ease. As she entered the room, she swore that next time (if there would even be a

next time) she would bring a friend. She moved about the
room; she found a drink. She saw some familiar faces but
interacted with no one. Occasionally a tentative smile
would leak out, and one caught the attention of an
attractive man. When his eyes caught hers for a moment,
he returned her smile, and turned to set down his drink.
He was about to ask her to dance. But Melanie's gaze
fell, first to the ice cubes still afloat in her drink
and then to the floor. She watched the man's feet turn
toward her and hesitate and then turn away.

❀

In a movie, a leading man might pursue the woman behind the
downcast eyes. But in real life, most men, not eager for rejection,
want encouragement. Melanie gave none.

Most self-defeating behavior that stems from inhibition involves
missed opportunities. They show up in all kinds of places, not just
singles parties: at work, at the mailbox, in a hardware store.
Anywhere.

Suzanne was not dressed to impress when she ran into
the hardware store to buy a few tools; she was, in fact,
somewhat sweaty from her attempts to install a garage
door opener. Nevertheless, he noticed her. He was tall,
he smelled good, and he looked like a man who could
handle tools. He was in the line behind her, studying
her purchase, when he inquired about what she was
working on. Embarrassed by her appearance, Suzanne
responded with only a brief factual report on her garage
door project. He said he was impressed that she was not
intimidated by mechanical things, as was his ex-wife.
But Suzanne remained unwilling to be known. She did not
mention that she had been working on her project all
morning and was about to scream with frustration. She
did not ask him if she had bought the right tools. She did

not ask him for anything. She paid her bill, and left.

❦

When a woman is ready for a man, she will notice an opportunity like this one and seize it if she finds the man desirable. Suzanne wasn't ready. She did not feel attractive; she wasn't prepared for male attention. It didn't even occur to her until later that he might be flirting with her. She was just taking care of business.

Sometimes the opportunity is more obvious, but not accessible at the moment. Today's woman often has to juggle her career, personal development, family, friends and her romantic attachments. It can be hard to prioritize.

> Diane had been hoping for weeks and weeks that her new neighbor would ask her to go out with him. Paul was attractive, friendly, and apparently unattached. She had just hung up the phone after making dinner plans with a girlfriend when he knocked at her door. The sight of him on her front steps gave her a thrill. Finally, he had noticed her. He began with an apology: "I hope you don't think me presumptuous to ask on such short notice, but I have just been offered two tickets to the opera tonight, and I thought it might give us a chance to get better acquainted. Are you interested?"
>
> Of course Diane was interested. But she was also nervous, and almost paralyzed for a moment. She sputtered, "I'm sorry, I have plans for tonight, and I'm afraid it would be too late to cancel." Paul was already turning away as he said, "Perhaps another time." Her tentative response, "Yes, perhaps . . ." may not have been heard.

❦

Diane's actions were not entirely self-defeating. Putting her prior commitment first conveyed self-esteem as well as a healthy respect for her woman friend. Unfortunately, that is as far as Diane could go; she abandoned the opportunity instead of making Paul a counteroffer. Another chronically single woman might defeat herself by playing hard to get, implying that her plans were with a man. Trying to spice things up with jealousy is not a good route to take; it's abusive and does not attract good men. It would also be self-defeating to cancel out on her friend for a date with the man; it would communicate poor self-esteem, or even desperation, which also do not attract good men. The best thing to do is to seek a way to extend the opportunity, on the assumption that you are worth waiting for. A positive message might be, "Unfortunately, I have plans with a girlfriend tonight. But I do hope you will invite me again. I would like to get to know you better."

A more aggressive message might be, "I am going out with a girlfriend tonight, but I'm free tomorrow. Can we do something tomorrow night?"

Whether you go for the subtle or the more aggressive way, you are communicating your interest, making yourself approachable, and reinforcing your self-esteem.

Some chronically single women defeat themselves by keeping conversations superficial when they could become personal and inviting — especially when they are caught off guard, or feeling insecure.

Pam was not prepared for the feelings triggered in her by the movie Fred had selected, and she was working hard to not let them show. She wanted to make a good impression and, as a member of a helping profession, she felt a special need to look healthy, emotionally as well as physically. Fred too had strong feelings triggered by the movie; his head filled with images of his long struggle with his father; his chest filled with breathless pain. All he could say was "Wow." But Pam, still intent on looking good, missed the cues on his face and in his voice. All she said was, "Yeah, wasn't that a great movie?" He made no

further effort to connect with her. The silence was
eventually broken by a discussion of other good movies
they had each seen.

❧

A door was opened through which they could see one another,
but the opportunity was missed, because Pam was caught up in her
shame. Pam might have shared some of her memories or feelings
with Fred and allowed him to see something of the richness of her
inner being, but she did not. And her unwillingness to share her
feelings may have left him with the impression that she was shallow. While mistakes like these are not always terminal to the relationship, they do tend to cool things off.

Yet another form of self-defeating behavior is being aloof. For
some women, this behavior is deliberate; many of us have been
taught that it is better to play at least a little hard to get. The old
theory, I suppose, was that men like, or even need, a little challenge. How many movies have you seen in which a man works hard
to get the attention of a woman and finally wins her, and they live
happily ever after? Hollywood! In real life, the story seldom ends
with the capture of the hard-won mate, for the man who loves the
challenge may actually love the chase better than the capture and
may disappear once the conquest is made.

Playing hard to get may be a familiar, though not necessarily
comfortable, place to hide. For the fear of being known, or the fear
of being rejected may cause a woman to behave in such a way that
she will not be known at all.

Linda had admired Hal for some time when he
happened to sit near her in the cafeteria. He was tall and
handsome and popular, and she was absolutely sure that
he could never be interested in her; he was totally out of
her league. Anxious to hide her interest in him, she
reached into her pocket for a wad of messages; she had
already read them, but she reread each one, trying to

appear quite concerned about what she was reading. He noticed her, but mindful of how busy she looked, he turned away and struck up a conversation with someone else.

❀

Being aloof gives the clear impression that you are too busy, or too snobbish, or too in love with someone else to bother with a relationship. It is a behavior designed to distance, and Linda will probably remain alone until she can reveal her interest in a man and let herself be known.

Women who carry a lot of fear and shame sometimes develop nervous habits that manifest themselves in the company of men, and so constitute yet another roadblock. Simple nervous habits, like giggling or twirling a lock of hair, may even add to your charm, but anxiety can create symptoms that are fundamentally disruptive to your interactions with men. Talking too much or telling your whole life story in the first twenty minutes clearly precludes a desirable progressive exposure. Some women become so paralyzed with fear that they are unable to speak or swallow, and some even become prey to anxiety attacks. It is awfully hard to make a good impression under circumstances like these.

Although attractive men usually made Toni nervous, she was not especially anxious when she first met Al. Though he was handsome, she did not feel threatened; he was just a nice guy who tended bar part-time in the restaurant frequented by the girls on Friday nights. Because she did not see him as eligible, Toni had no difficulty in making light conversation. Over time they became friendly, and even called each other once in a while.

The last phone call changed everything: Al began to discuss the demands of his restaurant. When Toni discovered that this part-time bartender owned the restaurant — that, in fact, he had excellent prospects —

her anxiety shot through the roof. Combined with good looks, a sharp mind, sensitivity, and an apparent interest in her, Al's financial security suddenly made him a threat. Toni reacted with so much anxiety that she heard the throbbing of her own pulse in her ear. She was glad Al could not see the beads of sweat breaking out on her forehead, or the trembling of her hands. She felt clammy, even faint, and extremely self-conscious. When she began to hyperventilate, Al asked, "Are you okay, Toni? Is something wrong?" She wanted to say "No, I'm fine" and go on with their conversation, but she could not. She finally caught her breath and sputtered, "May I call you back tomorrow?" Al said "Sure," but tomorrow never came, and he never asked why.

❀

Toni's opportunity was cut short not only by her anxiety attack but also by the shame that prevented her from explaining herself to Al. While severe anxiety may require professional treatment, its potentially devastating effect on romance can often be averted by some open sharing.

On the flip side of inhibition is the habit of demeaning oneself. Going on about your flaws may summon a reassuring compliment or two, but sooner or later people tire of the game.

Bunni was pleased to be invited to the baseball game with the gang from work; she was fairly new on the job and didn't know anyone well. She was interested in one man, who was not so much handsome as he was sure of himself. That made him attractive to her.

Because she had never been to the stadium before, Bunni arrived a little early; she found her seat and began to read the program. As others arrived, she noticed that she was dressed too formally — out of step with the cutoffs, torn jeans, and baggy t-shirts her co-workers wore. As the man of her dreams sat in the seat directly

in front of her, Bunni's monologue began. "I don't know
what's wrong with me. I should have gone home to change
clothes." Despite their protestations, she continued,
"You all look so sporty. I feel like an old lady. Maybe
if I bought myself a baseball cap, I would fit in."

❀

Although initial reactions to Bunni were supportive, her new
friends got tired of her neediness. They found it draining, and they
began to ignore her, fulfilling her worst fears.

Many chronically single women feel completely miserable at
times; loneliness, frustration, and even despair may surface now
and then and create a sense of depression. Some women, however,
suffer from a clinical depression that has preceded and perhaps
caused their difficulties with men. Their lack of interest in connecting with others and their depressive symptoms turn people off.

Nellie arrived for the workshop wearing old jeans and a
beige polo shirt that seemed to fade into her pale flesh.
She was almost completely devoid of color. Although she
did have on make-up, it appeared to be old, like her
jeans. Her hair was oily and stringy, and it was obvious
that Nellie was not taking good care of herself these
days. As the women began to introduce themselves and
discuss their reasons for attending the workshop, Nellie
shifted in her seat and her heavy sighs could be heard
across the room. Eventually, it was her turn, and she
said "I don't know why I'm here. What is the point? I've
given up on men."

❀

Nellie needed treatment for depression. Not an especially heavy
woman to begin with, she had lost 16 pounds over the past few
months; she wasn't eating well and wasn't sleeping either.
Although she attributed her depression to her bad luck with men,

her history suggested that the opposite was true — her untreated depression was killing relationships. A combination of medication and psychotherapy soon restored the color to her social life as well as her cheeks.

Probably the ultimate form of inhibition is avoidance. While moderate inhibition can cause a woman to avoid eye contact or opportunities to get closer to others, a more severe inhibition that causes a woman to avoid relationships altogether may stem from a phobia.

> Unable to cope with the interpersonal conflicts in the office, Sabrina had quit her job and formed a word-processing business in her home. She designed her own advertising materials and launched a successful marketing campaign from home. Her only work related contact consisted of picking up and delivering work, and this was tolerable. But, oh, how she looked forward to being home again, with her Siamese cat and her cozy fireplace and the total absence of others.

❦

It had been a long time since Sabrina's avoidance of relationships had caused her any conscious pain, but the death of her cat put Sabrina in enough pain to seek change. This one relationship had survived her deepest retreat and when it was ripped away from her by a speeding motorist, Sabrina's pain was ripped open, too. Now it could be addressed. Although Sabrina's retreat was about pain, a fear of pain, and a related inhibition, a severe retreat from social life often represents a phobia, for which professional treatment is available.

While chronically single women do not always have pets, this is certainly the stereotype. In Sabrina's case, the cat symbolized the relationship she desired but avoided. For other women, the cat may be a teacher, enabling an inhibited woman to experience love and attachment, which can be transferred to human relationships when the woman is ready — hopefully, without losing the cat.

# 2

# *False Advertising*

Do you, like the ad man, aim at quick sales? The immediate impression, the image that will jump from the page? Do you come center stage in a mask?

A mask may work well on a stage, when it may be desirable to exaggerate one aspect of a character for dramatic effect, but not in real life. It is likely to attract a man who would not want a relationship with the real you and to put off the one who would be attracted to exactly those qualities that are hidden.

The human personality is complex: it is made up of many traits. Some may be negative and others positive; some may be aggressive and others receptive. A hot temper, for example, combined with compassion, may produce healthy assertive behavior. Together, they work well. But temper alone can be harsh, and compassion alone can say, "wimp."

Part of human development is the progressive integration of personality traits and the concomitantly progressive ability to respond and take action from an integrated core. But when this process stops short and integration does not take place, the personality remains compartmentalized, much like an ice tray with traits separated into cubes. In such cases the easiest course of action is to "wear" one trait at a time, like a mask.

One of the most common masks is that of the Sex Goddess or Whore, a very effective persona for attracting a lot of attention from men, especially in nightclubs. Unfortunately, it only attracts sexual attention, and so often attracts sex addicts.

> Melinda let one leg drop as she lighted on the bar stool, forcing open the slit in the front of her silky skirt. There could have been no more obvious directional signal, and the man beside her didn't notice her face. He approached her and then asked her name. It was all he needed to know.
>
> Three dates later, all devoted to sex, Melinda was asking Martin sadly where their relationship was going — and he was dumbfounded. He was engaged to someone else, who was away at college. He had accepted a simple invitation to a sexual spree.

❧

Melinda *was* sexually attractive, as she knew all too well, having been sexually abused as a child. Now, though, as she enjoyed the power of control, she overlooked her need to be seen as a bright and sensitive woman, well advanced in a good career and lot more complex than she appeared.

A very different but also common mask is that of the Brain, rather dry, and though interesting, unlikely to attract many men.

> Eleanor had been looking forward to meeting John for some time. She had heard a lot about him, and she expected they would have a lot in common. Moreover, he was rumored to be the most eligible bachelor in the company. He was relocating and eager to make new connections.

For their first meeting Eleanor wore a straight gray suit, and though the small red handkerchief in her breast pocket suggested her inner color, it was effectively hidden. She shook his hand heartily and began to talk of his work on a project she had evaluated the previous year. When he invited her to lunch, she was very pleased. She thought they were on a date, until he asked whether her secretary was married.

❀

Clearly the Brain does not attract men to her as a woman, even when physically and emotionally attractive, as Eleanor was; the Brain calls their attention to issues. Sometimes she attracts other brains, but more often she attracts little boys who want her to figure things out for them.

The Brain — on the opposite side of the coin where the Sex Goddess lolls — is also concerned with her body, but uses her intelligence to draw attention away from it. The Sex Goddess and the Brain may have been sexually abused as children, and by saying "Don't touch," they feel as if they have power over the men who were guilty of molesting them.

Another mask that practically guarantees a lack of male attention is that of the Prude. An overactive conscience, combined with a preoccupation about others, produces this distancing mask.

Throughout her life, Harriet had always been told she looked older than her age. This may have sounded good when she was eleven and wanted to be a teenager, but now, at fifty-five, she was not delighted. Part of the trouble was the manner of her dress; she liked polyester and ordered tailored clothing from a catalog. Basically it was her "old" attitude and it showed in her face — the lines that had permanent residence on her forehead, the angled brow, the way her face seemed to come to a point at her lips.

When Harold moved into her apartment complex, Harriet took note. He was at least her age and had a handsome face, but she didn't like the way he wore his shirt collar open or the little sports car he drove. When she spotted him in the hot tub with a woman who was only forty, Harriet had a fit.

❊

A fit is probably all Harriet will ever have, for the Prude who is constantly withholding herself and never withholding her negative judgements does not make friends or find lovers. It is clear that such a deep-seated need to put others down has stemmed from a deep-seated hurt that calls for an open airing.

Very different from the mask of the Brain or the Prude is the mask of the Little Girl, or the Helpless Princess, loath to be seen as a complete woman.

It had been a long day at work, and Jan was tired, looking forward to getting home to her comforts. She was not amused when she found her battery dead. As she sat behind the wheel, she tested the ignition again and again in anger and disbelief, swearing under her breath. Her demeanor entirely changed when a man approached her car. Her tight, angry mouth softened and pouted a little; in addition, her lower lip began to quiver. Even her spine seemed to soften, as she allowed her body to fall back into the full support of the seat. Help had arrived — and Jan was not about to suggest she was anything but helpless or to make reference to being tired from a job.

The parking lot encounter bloomed into a courtship, and in the early months Jan was sure she had found Mr. Right — attentive and sensitive, and always there to meet every need. As the months slipped by, however, the mask slipped away and so did Mr. Right, for he saw beneath her false advertising to the competent woman she was.

❊

Jan fears that men will be intimidated by her strength, and so wears her needier qualities around them. She is learning that in order to attract men who are not afraid of female strength, she needs to show her strength along with her other qualities.

The woman who wears the mask of the Little Girl or the Helpless Princess can attract men who have a strong need to take care of a woman, but who ultimately need her neediness. Initially a woman may enjoy this kind of attention and even thrive on it, but playing a role is tiresome. And sooner or later this grown woman will find the fatherly character controlling.

The mask of the Little Girl is most often worn to placate the inner needy child of a woman insufficiently loved by her father. And the Little Princess has perhaps been spoiled and wants more. So the role of a child is portrayed, and the woman attracts Mr. Wrong.

Another mask that hides competence in women is that of the Airhead, also known as the Clutz, more adolescent than childlike; she often unwittingly attracts attention to her body and is then unable to respond.

> Polly's well-earned position on the corporate ladder and her political acumen invited respect — but the giggle could be heard throughout the office. Anyone who had worked there longer than two weeks knew the giggle meant that a man had stopped at her desk. Usually a representative of a local firm or a co-worker, but today it was a company executive visiting from out of town. He didn't seem to mind when she dropped the report she had prepared for their conference. He bent down with her to collect the papers, and she knew he enjoyed the cleavage in the midst of the soft folds of her blouse. Shaken by being seen as a woman, Polly giggled again and said, "Gee, Mr. Thompson, I'm all fingers today."

❀

She meant, of course, all thumbs.

Of necessity the adolescent Airhead who wanted fatherly attention had put Mr. Thompson off, for his sexual interest felt incestuous to her. Only once in the past year had Polly been able to establish a relationship with a man — an almost asexual one with a
would-be big brother who wanted control. She had to become willing to show men her intelligence, along with her other qualities.

Brotherly attention is often the result of another kind of mask,
called One of the Guys. This mask appears when a woman over-
identifies with men, squelching some of her most attractive qualities.

> Deb was the only woman at the pool, in the company of
> four men who were all spoken for. As the beer cans went
> round, Deb saw a chance to join in — and found herself
> then in the midst of complaints about wives. "Most women
> don't understand what men are about," she found herself
> saying.
> Being "in" felt good, and so did the beer that went to
> her head as she joined in the game of debunking the
> women who came to the pool — for flat chests or fat
> thighs or any remarkable thing. Then men became targets,
> and Deb led the attack on a new man who had come to
> the pool with some books. Despite his handsome
> appearance, she took him to be a real dud and gleefully
> said so to the guys. Even in her drunken fog, her
> disappointment overwhelmed her when the dud invited
> someone else to the hot tub.
> These guys really liked Deb; they even expressed a wish
> that their wives could be a little more like her. Of note,
> however, none of the four men had chosen women who
> would guzzle beer with them. They might have been
> interested in an affair with Deb, but none had chosen a
> woman like her as their mate.

Most women who put on the mask of One of the Guys are afraid of intimacy and cover their stifled fears. Some cover their fears with behavior like Deb's. She sometimes slept with married men like those at the pool. And just as she had tolerated listening to their abuse of women at the pool, she tolerated accounts of their sexual fantasies and exploits. It took Deb a long time to see the abuse inherent in their treatment of her and the impact it had on her growing ambivalence about intimacy. Ironically, it was through hanging out with women that Deb eventually attracted some wholesome male attention.

Another mask that can be popular with some men is that of the Comedienne; like the mask of One of the Guys, this usually leads no further than platonic relationships or brief and superficial affairs.

Connie had enjoyed a good sense of humor as long as she could remember. She loved to make people laugh and was often the life of the party. This party was no exception. Still she was vaguely aware of her nervousness as she monitored the door to see if Jeff, the handsome new man at the shop, would show up. She continued to circulate, however, and to amuse everyone with jokes and clever remarks, most of which related to not having a date. No one was spared. Not even Jeff, who had finally arrived and approached her warmly with a bottle of wine to share. As she tugged on his colorful tie, she asked if he was trying to make a fashion statement. Her comment was meant in fun, he was sure, and he laughed — but he also moved on.

Most of Connie's male friends enjoyed her, but they did not ask her for dates, they did not take her seriously. Some seemed really to respond to her humor, but relationships with them turned out not to be fulfilling. Some were depressed, and some passive, and as they depended on her humor for stimulation, she found their dependency draining. Sometimes these relationships did survive, but her male audience would eventually move on to someone more entertaining when her own underlying depression became evident.

While humor is often said to mask anger, it can mask anything — including fear, anxiety, or pain. For Connie, it was usually self-demeaning, suggestive of underlying pain; on the night of the party, however, it sounded sarcastic, suggestive of anger. Dealing with the feelings underneath the humorous facade will help this woman to be taken more seriously and to be appreciated.

Another mask that often draws platonic admiration from men is that of the Trooper, also known as the Big Sister. The Trooper/Big Sister can handle anything, and others will usually let her. She has genuine strength, but she uses an inflated sense of responsibility to cover her own emotional needs.

> Sally had just gone to sleep after watching the late show when the phone startled her awake. This was the third time in a year that Rick had called her in the middle of the night, faced with a romantic crisis. She was a specialist in resolving his problems with girlfriends who had thrown him out on the street. "Sure, come on over," she said. "I'll put on some tea."
>
> The tea, at least, was for Sally, as she listened to Rick until dawn. For Rick there was rest on her sofa and the enjoyment of pancakes to boot. He would spend the night on her sofa, and call his girlfriend while Sally made breakfast. But Sally found little enjoyment in his sweet-talking phone call to his girlfriend as she washed up the dishes.

❦

Troopers are attractive to users — little boys who need a big sister or a mommy to help them out, but, like Sally, they know they are being used. Sally knew who Rick was, but lived on the fantasy that some day he would look at her in a new light and fall desperately in love: they would help one another overcome their emotional handicaps and live happily ever after. Now that Sally has begun to deal with her own emotional problems, her need to wait for this little boy is beginning to fade, and she will look for a partner to meet the needs that have been too long suppressed.

Another mask that projects strength is that of the Amazon. Like the Trooper, the woman who wears this mask appears to be able to handle anything. She is different, however, in her motivation. While the Trooper acts as the benevolent sister, trying to earn love through good deeds, the Amazon acts as the self-sufficient powerhouse, trying to replace men. She is independent, in the extreme, and she tends to be harshly critical of men.

> It had been a long time since Ariel had allowed anyone to help her with anything. Although she had only average intelligence, sheer determination had enabled her to surpass her limitations — in her education, on the job, in the business she developed, and even in household repairs. She was a human dynamo.
> While waxing her car one day, Ariel noticed the attention of the new neighbor. He looked capable, too, and she admired that. His physical strength and prominent chin and full lips were attractive. He came over to get acquainted, and she was pleased. They talked amicably about his move to the condo and the affairs of the homeowners group. And then he began to take note of her car. When he expressed some concern about the low tread on her tires, she sniped, "Thanks for sharing."

One blast of verbal gunfire is usually enough to terminate new relationships, and so it was with Ariel and her neighbor. He now knows better than to share his observations with her; Ariel knows best.

Ariel was the daughter of alcoholics and was the oldest of seven children. It was Ariel on whom their survival depended; for their needs as well as her own, there was nowhere to turn but to her. Now that the siblings are grown up and long gone, Ariel is alone. In her forties, she is still the lone warrior, guarding against a danger that no longer exists.

Although the Amazon's verbal gunfire tends to terminate male attention, as happened in Ariel's case, it may lure a man who likes challenge or a man whose inner child wants mommy. Happy endings can come from Amazons who let down their guard and express some of their needs.

Another mask that is not popular with men, though strangely attractive to some, is the Bitch, who is sometimes called the Critic. This woman is usually just as hard on herself as on others — but she is surely known for being hard to please.

> They had shared a long, full evening of entertainment and were on their way to Helen's place for a nightcap when she began to be annoyed by his driving. First he cut a traffic signal too close for her comfort; she didn't comment. Then he braked suddenly; she grabbed the dashboard. She was trying. But once he got on the freeway and hit a few of the disks that separate the lanes, Helen could not restrain herself. "Hasn't anyone ever told you how annoying it is to ride on those bumps?" she scolded. Her voice was loud and harsh and reminded him of her earlier complaints: the salad dressing, too much; the parking attendant, too young; the movie plot, too thin. Fed up, he hit every disk he could see, and then needed that drink when they got to her place — but did not want to share it with Helen.

❧

Helen had been nervous since the start of the evening. On her first date since her husband's death, she was somewhat fearful to be with a stranger. As the time for the nightcap approached, her fear became terror. She didn't want to think about it so she thought about his driving and let the Bitch take over to protect her in her vulnerability.

Few men are attracted to the Bitch or the Critic, for anger is not an emotion that draws people in. Sometimes guilt-ridden bad boys who want to be scolded are attracted, and sometimes a passive-aggressive disk-bumper, who's hardly a joy. But the Bitch has actually few chances to meet men, for society in general finds anger in women even more unacceptable than in men.

Bitches and Critics are often frightened and ashamed and confused by their anger. Recovery requires dealing with the feelings hiding beneath it. And Helen began by talking about her fears with her next date.

Although the mask of the Bitch turns men off, no mask can do it so well as that of the Bride-in-Waiting. This woman is more focused on getting married than on finding a mate, and for her, the wedding is more important than the groom. Timid men can sometimes be led by the nose by such women but seldom to the altar — though sometimes the pointless illusion can go on for years.

Jim was pleased when Annie asked him out; he associated her boldness with the strength he had admired in his mother and sister. He was not so pleased when she came on to him so strongly on their first date, and he was outright shocked when she produced condoms from her wallet. With considerable hesitation, he nevertheless succumbed to her advances, and the affair began. The next morning he was full of regret for his uncharacteristic behavior. He was about to apologize when he found himself hearing a declaration of love from Annie. He could not believe his ears and he felt a little queasy as he made it to the street.

❀

Even men who are queasy at being taken over will sometimes pursue and ask for a date, as Jim did. For him it was guilt at the start, but there was something heady about being adored. Then after three months, the date was set for the marriage. The minister was talked to, the guests listed, the dress ordered — and it all seemed unreal. Having felt an absence of substance from the start, Jim suddenly saw himself as the object he was to Annie: the essential ingredient of her wedding, and it never took place.

Annie had been excited about weddings since she was a little girl and she became desperate for a wedding of her own. At thirty-five, she cherished a videotape of Princess Di's wedding and knew that she too wanted a long train on her dress. It was her obsession about the ceremony, but also her sense of desperation about making this event happen in her own life, that scared Jim away. Desperation to be married tends to distance men. When the Bride-in-Waiting manages to get a relationship started, it is not unusual to find that the potential groom is afraid of commitment; the dance that ensues can last for years, make both parties feel crazy, and often does not lead to marriage. Annie, unfortunately, went through two broken engagements before exploring her desperation to be married. When her desperation quieted, she found her mate.

The Phantom mask can also lead to fruitless engagements by attracting men who are afraid of commitment. The Phantom seems elusive and hard to pin down. Her elusiveness will be attractive to some, perhaps to many; but the attraction will not lead to many courtships. If she is physically attractive, men will probably be curious about her, but they will see by her mask she is difficult to know, and they will not expect to connect. To most men this woman gives the impression that she is completely self-fulfilled, snobbish, or out of reach; she is the ideal love object for the man who is afraid of intimacy. Some will be content to love her from afar, and some will dream of being that special man for whom the Phantom will finally reveal herself. They will want to see the butterfly freed from the cocoon.

Hillary was far and away the most beautiful woman he had ever seen. From the moment she entered the room,

his attention was on her, and he knew immediately she
was unattached. She seemed to float above the ground in
a way that charmed him, and her palpable separateness
was mysteriously alluring. He had seen creatures like her
in his dreams but had not won their attention. This
woman he would dream of tonight.

Hillary was not in therapy; the dreamer was — a chronically single man who entered therapy to deal with issues of intimacy. When
he had a second chance to become acquainted with Hillary, he was
ready to take a risk. He found her to be cold and slippery at first
encounter, but he was determined to know her mystery, to see the
butterfly arise from the cocoon. It was a wish that would never be
fulfilled, for as he grew healthier, his need to attach himself to
Phantoms faded and he began to dream of lovers.

Hillary, unwilling to look inside the cocoon herself, had remained
unwilling to be known. She has yet to come to terms with her fear
of what's hidden inside.

Finally, there is the mask of the Ghost. Beyond making a woman
mysterious, this mask makes her invisible. Wearing the mask, she
can simply disappear, for she is expressionless and devoid of energy; she can easily pass through a room unnoticed. Her efforts to
speak up while wearing the mask frequently result in being interrupted or ignored outright. The Ghost mask neither attracts nor
repels men; it keeps the woman's existence a secret.

Amanda had usually avoided the weekly night out with
the girls at the office, but one night she was thirsting on
many levels. Not noticing her, the women she knew took
seats at the bar, and Amanda, of necessity, took a seat
between two strangers. She felt her spirit evaporate. As
she tried to make conversation, the women seemed always
to be talking with someone else. She was feeling about
four years old, but she ordered a gin and tonic and then

looked at the band. Soon the others would all be dancing, and perhaps she could leave unnoticed.

❀

Actually, she could have left unnoticed at any time. She was barely there to begin with. Amanda had been incestuously abused as a child and was hiding; she was still the little child who felt trapped. Amanda's early recovery involved getting angry at others who would ignore her and treat her like a ghost; soon after, it involved identifying other little boys and girls to talk to. Her eventual success in making herself visible and attractive, however, involved owning the Ghost as her own projection, and understanding its job in her life as an incest survivor. Once the secret was out, Amanda no longer needed to hide. No longer hidden, she attracted ample attention.

Women sometimes don masks deliberately in an attempt to control the kind of attention they get, and for good reason. Certainly there are work and social environments in which it is prudent to reveal only limited information about yourself. And some jobs encourage a woman to project a certain image: a cocktail waitress will get better tips as a Whore than a Brain; a physician gets more referrals as a Trooper than a Bitch. But in a social environment a masked woman is most often protecting herself out of fear, though sometimes she's acting on misinformation about what is attractive to men.

Wearing a mask may be a habit more than a choice. In such cases recovery usually requires not only a full awareness of the mask but also a deeper look at its purpose. In the process, a mask may be found to be dreadfully unattractive, so it is important to remember it is a distortion of an asset — and recovery is not about eliminating masks but about integrating them with the valuable traits underneath. Once this is accomplished, a woman can fully employ her many inner resources in her search for a mate.

# 3

# *Transitional Partners*

Loneliness, or the fear of it, can motivate a single woman to make some interesting choices in boyfriends — including men she could not, or would not, stay with. Even relationships that can't last may sound better to her than being alone. Once in a great while, of course, a miracle happens, and a relationship like this becomes permanent. More often, however, these transitional relationships become part of the problem. Part of what keeps a woman chronically single is her attachment to partners who are not available to her, or acceptable to her, for a committed, long-term relationship.

When a woman begins a new relationship knowing it won't last, and perhaps even hoping it won't, it may well be that she is giving herself an opportunity to work through some unresolved issue. She may need to work through a hurt or disappointment; she may need to learn to accept others as they are. So long as she continues to view the relationship as temporary — as transitional, as serving a particular purpose in her life — it can be a positive growth experience.

Sometimes, however, what started as a temporary arrangement begins to turn into a more permanent attachment. A woman may enter a transitional relationship only to gratify social and sexual needs and then find that her behavior is in conflict with her values. She will then need to make him fit. The woman begins to delude herself into thinking the unavailable man will somehow become available, the inappropriate man will change.

Becoming lost in such fantasies is not uncommon among chronically single women, for many have an unconscious need to change men and are thus instinctively attracted to men they can hope to improve.

Although she may think she will be free when she gets a man to change, freedom actually is won through accepting others the way they are. Getting there may require grieving the loss of her father's attention, as that is what this woman is typically acting out. It also requires some confidence that someone else will be there for her if she lets go of a man who really doesn't fit her life. Fear of being alone motivates many women to do time with "fixer-uppers" that they have no intention of accepting as is.

For other women, these hopeless relationships may actually signify progress. When a woman is beginning to learn new behaviors, she may inadvertently get involved with one more unavailable man for the purpose of practicing her new skills. As her healing is completed, one of two things will usually happen: he will become more available, or he will become easier to leave.

For some women attachment to unavailable partners is chronic, for when a woman has an unconscious need to remain single, she will naturally seek the company of men who will not represent a serious challenge to her marital status. While avowing a desire to form a healthy, committed, intimate relationship, she is actually defeating herself.

It's curious that so many women can delude themselves into believing that married men are available when it is well known that even those who promise to divorce their wives seldom do. Those who do then face the challenge of establishing trust, knowing that both are capable of deceit. Yet this struggle will attract many.

> Although it would be some time before Carrie admitted it, she knew from the first that Rick was married. He did not wear a wedding ring, but she knew the signs all too well: not offering his home phone number, looking frequently at his watch, asking her to meet him for an early dinner on a week night, and paying in cash. But it was more than the signs; she just knew he was cheating on someone. Carrie did not ask, however, and Rick did not volunteer the information until sex was imminent. By then she didn't care. She thanked him for his honesty, and the affair began. Rick thought he had finally found a woman who would understand him, and Carrie thought she had finally found a man who would appreciate her.

❀

In his own way, Rick did appreciate her. He especially appreciated her no-strings approach to the affair. He was looking for outside support to make his marriage tolerable; he had no intention of ending it. Rationalizing her fear of commitment, Carrie claimed to want only good company. But she found she wanted more and ended the affair after six months.

Like Carrie, some women habitually play the role of the other woman, motivated by ambivalence, unresolved fear of commitment, or a need to continue some childhood drama, such as a daughter's wish to steal Daddy away from Mommy. It is only when the motive is exposed that recovery is possible.

Almost as patently unavailable as married men are confirmed bachelors. Some who are sought after by hostesses as single men or by single women as escorts are clearly enjoying an active social life; some, on the other hand, enjoy quiet and privacy.

> On his first date with Lynn, Philip said plainly, "I am

not the marrying kind. I have seen marriage ruin too many good relationships." Lynn chose to believe he was just waiting for the right girl. He was thirty-eight; he was a successful businessman and an animal rights activist; he was handsome and athletic; he had never married. After a while they agreed on a commitment to a monogamous intimate relationship, one day at a time. Carrie saw the relationship in that light — but her friends expressed concern about her growing expectations.

Despite their commitment, Philip seldom asked Lynn to go out — and then it was to some such formal affair as a special charity benefit. She missed the private times she had spent with other men, sharing a pizza while watching a basketball game on TV or just snuggling after a hard day's work. It was three years before Lynn even acknowledged her disappointment and frustration and asked Philip to get professional help in overcoming his fear of commitment to marriage. He was shocked. He was happy as things were. However, a gentleman to the last, he withdrew from her life to allow her to seek the mate she said she wanted.

❦

How unfortunate that it took Carrie three years to believe what Philip had said on their first date. Indeed, Carrie did want a mate; she had no intention of being a lifetime bachelorette. But her behavior suggests she wanted to get married on the installment plan. She was putting it off.

Some men *are* unavailable because they are afraid of commitment — and it is not hard to identify them, unless unresolved issues block the view. It is frequently women who have been neglected by their fathers who are attracted to these men, for it is so much easier to follow a familiar pattern — to keep trying to gain attention rather than to change. Instead, any attempts to hasten this man's pace will usually be matched with an equal amount of resistance.

At thirty-two Jason was serving as groomsman for the second time. As he dressed for the occasion, he noticed how good he looked in his tux; his imagination began to stir with fantasies of his own wedding. Maybe someday he would give marriage a try; today, it sounded like a good idea. In her bridesmaid's gown, Ellen was radiant as she walked down the long church aisle, and Jason could easily imagine her as the bride. He approached her at the reception. He said nothing, but he took her hand and led her to the dance floor. Romantic music and champagne intoxicated them, and before long, both were whispering dreamily about their turn at the altar. Jason made sure to get her phone number before saying goodnight, since he fully intended to reel her in. He told her he would call her in a couple of days.

After a week Ellen began to wonder whether Jason had been serious about wanting to see her. She remembered the name of the company he worked for and telephoned, trying hard to make her call sound like a casual follow-up. But it could never sound casual to Jason; he began to feel panic when his secretary said Ellen was on the line.

After collecting himself, Jason lifted the receiver. He, too, tried to sound casual — but very busy. He promised to call later in the week, perhaps to make plans for the weekend. Ellen was again optimistic. Before the evening had passed, she had posted a notecard expressing her delight in meeting such a wonderful guy. It blew him away, and, of course, he never called.

❀

Commitment phobic men are often very attractive to women with poor self-esteem — especially women who were abandoned or neglected by their fathers. These women often measure their worth by their successes or failures with men. The hard work involved in trying to earn sustained attention of a man may seem quite natural to the woman neglected by her father; she has learned well that nothing comes easily.

Ellen gave up early, a good sign. She knew, at least, that as an adult she could look elsewhere for attention. She learned to look inside for the completion of her grief about her father, and to let men do half the work.

A relationship with an older man can be a convenient venue for working out certain unresolved issues. But it can also be a trap if the man takes the place of an ideal fantasy father.

> They met while sunbathing beside the apartment complex pool. Louise was grading a stack of papers completed by her third-grade class, and Eric was reading a book on do-it-yourself divorce. He looked so worldly that Louise was surprised he needed a manual for anything. He was bright and articulate, and she imagined a world of experience hidden in the folds of his skin. He was nearly twenty years her senior, but it didn't seem to matter to her. Around him she did not have to act self-assured; she could be herself.

❀

Eric and Louise dated steadily for two years, and on and off for another two. The first six months of their relationship was wonderful for Louise. Eric helped her discover a side of herself she had not known, and the relationship softened and enriched her personality. Unfortunately, Eric was uncomfortable with the age difference. Although he never left Louise, he repeatedly encouraged her to leave him. Though she had gained so much in only six months, Louise wanted more from her fantasy father. It took her four years to let go.

If a man is twenty or more years a woman's senior, their relationship is likely to involve some reenactment of the woman's relationship with her father. Even when the man is only ten years her senior, it is not unusual to find some shadows of the father-daughter relationship or her make-believe relationship with her fantasy father. An older man may be everything a woman wished her father could have been: experienced, attentive, and divorced.

Relationships with younger men are becoming more common, though not necessarily more acceptable. Women often struggle with severe guilt feelings over their attraction to younger men. It is still unusual to find a woman seriously involved with a man more than ten years her junior. The woman involved with a younger man may have difficulty committing to the relationship and some legitimate concerns about the welfare of her junior partner. Some women will fret about *his* ambivalence (he may have some), and seek his constant reassurance, rather than face her own qualms about dating a younger man. As with older men, it is the presence and intensity of those qualms that determine whether or not she is wasting time.

Relationships with emotionally unavailable men are common among chronically single women, and are commonly fruitless and frustrating. Since these men do not engage themselves in relationships, they offer no opportunity for growth; they may be inhibited by shame or just plain selfish, but often they are too immature to have a self to share. Nevertheless, many women maintain relationships with such men over long periods of time, usually out of fear of loneliness.

> This time, Claire was certain that she had not chosen another emotionally unavailable man. Ben was easily the most romantic man she had ever met. In the week between their first and second dates, he phoned her almost every night at bedtime, often talking for an hour or more. He talked with her about his struggle with issues from the past and about his dreams for the future. And always, always, he wanted to know more about her. For a full month, there was a card from Ben in Claire's mailbox almost every day, and a flower in his hand at every date. Claire couldn't have been happier.
>
> Ben's attentions then began to fall off. By the end of two months, what had been a courtship amounted to little more than lying on her couch and watching television. It was her couch he was lying on, and it was the TV that had

his passive attention; he was offering nothing. When Claire
at last complained of his lack of attention to her, he
answered with a complaint that she was needy. Claire
began to fear that she had found another emotionally
needy man.

✴

Claire was right. Ben had spent all his romantic assets in the
first few weeks. He was an emotionally unavailable man in a very
clever disguise and he had no inner resources. Ben was right, too.
Claire was needy, and it was her neediness that had made him
attractive to her in the first place. She had entered the relationship
starved for attention. Knowing only the hunger of the poor, she
assumed such a toast of attention to be the daily fare of the more
well-to-do; it did not occur to her that Ben's behavior was sympto-
matic of his own neediness and his insecurity and anxiety.
Excessiveness in anything — even romance — is a bad sign.

Some immature, emotionally unavailable men are conspicuously
narcissistic and characteristically display such traits as grandiosity,
interpersonal exploitation, a sense of terminal uniqueness, unrealistic expectations about love, and an attitude of entitlement, among
others. They are not infrequently addicts, but those problems are
often obscured by their boyish sense of fun and romantic talk about
ideal love, which can be very appealing initially.

Darrel could write poetry only when he was half loaded.
For several years he had managed to make a decent living
writing and selling precious messages from his heart, only
heard when he was under the influence. Darrel's drink
was gin. Rosie met him in a local pub, where Darrel
occasionally read his works to an eager audience. From
the start his poetry showed her a sad, lonely little boy
inside; it was that little boy in Darrel that attracted Rosie.
Soon she became his playmate, laughing and drinking and
frolicking with him. Before long she was his mother, loving
and supporting him and making his excuses when he was

too loaded to read or write. Eventually, she was his harshest critic, nagging and scolding him, and wanting him to grow up.

❀

Little boys can be very hard to leave, but Rosie did. Seeing that he was no better off with her in his life, she managed to walk away from him. Only then did Rosie begin to look at herself, raising good questions about why she would choose a boy for a mate. Finally, focusing on her own issues rather than on his problems, she has been able to connect with more mature men who take responsibility for themselves.

Just as addiction is often a symptom of immaturity — of an inability to assume the responsibilities of an adult relationship — so is chronic unemployment. While there is nothing inherently wrong with a woman's choosing to provide financial support for a man or earning more than her mate, the red flags go up when she is always talking about his potential and he is doing nothing about it. What passes for a relationship then is usually a form of adoption.

At one time Andy had had a promising career in computer programming. Although it gave him a decent income, it did not give him satisfaction. He decided to go back to college — and he returned to his mother's home, where he would be supported through a second college education. It was at college that he and Theresa met, while she was pursuing an advanced degree in nursing. They had a psych class together and often sat on the grass outside the Humanities building after class to share their thoughts about the lecture. She was attracted to his wavy hair and the way the wind made those waves so wild. There was a freshness about Andy she envied; he seemed a free spirit. He was attracted to her eyes, and the way they seemed to see into people; she seemed to possess a wisdom beyond her years, and Andy felt safe in her presence.

Those eyes eventually saw Andy's reluctance to grow up. She might have rejected him at that point, but, instead she told herself that because of his great self-awareness, he had great potential. Her initial investment in that potential was limited to the favor of her company and her emotional support. As their relationship progressed, she replaced his mother, encouraging Andy in his studies, paying some of his expenses and sharing her home with him. Ultimately, Theresa fully invested herself, picking up responsibility for Andy's welfare, volunteering to be his conscience, and making herself the victim of his failures.

❦

Fortunately, Andy and Theresa saw early the need to deal with their conflicts around money. At this point, some couples find out that the woman's concern about his income is really a concern about what others are going to think. When worked through, sometimes this couple can shirk society's message and find peace as a family with the woman as the primary bread winner.

In Theresa's case, however, her concern was for herself, not for popular opinion. She did not want to support a man. This relationship worked out because each was willing to look at their own half of this mutual dependency and take responsibility for fulfilling their own dreams. And their dreams were compatible.

Some men who are perfectly capable of a mature relationship are nevertheless emotionally unavailable because their hearts are elsewhere. Men who are on the rebound may appear to be available, but beware.

The first thing Tim noticed about Laura was her gentle laugh; Laura was charmed by his smile and his dimples, and pleased to hear him say he was enjoying himself for the first time since his divorce. Over the early months of their courtship, he grew to love her sense of humor; how refreshing it was, he told Laura, after those last humorless years with his ex-wife. When he first complained about his ex-wife, Laura was pleased to be so favorably compared with a woman she saw as an enemy. Still, Tim's complaints about his wife began to tire her, as did trying to find some humorous angle on the situation to regain his attention. Finally, it wasn't funny anymore.

❀

Laura had been involved in many relationships with men — all of which had lasted no longer than a few months. Since all these men had had at least one long-term relationship with another woman, Laura felt she must be responsible for the break-up and sought help in learning how to keep a man's attention. It had not occurred to her she was choosing preoccupied men — unavailable men — unconsciously perpetuating her childhood experience of living in her mother's shadow. Given this insight, she came out into the light, where she eventually found her Mr. Right.

Though a bisexual man can be a good mate if he understands his sexual identity and is clear with you about expressing his sexuality, the man who is confused about his sexual identity is a poor candidate. Besides the increased danger of contracting AIDS, a woman takes a risk of not getting her emotional needs met with a man who cannot determine for himself what his needs are.

> Bryan had never had an intimate relationship with a man, unless you count the eye contact exchanged with a boy in the shower after gym class in junior high school. Bryan did count it, and often struggled with the desire he had felt in himself gazing into the other boy's eyes. Although years had passed, along with many relationships with women, Bryan at twenty-eight was feeling the pressure to determine his sexual identity once and for all. At thirty, Delia felt pressure, too, and during her three-year relationship with Bryan, she had regularly

shared her feelings about it with him. She wanted to be
accepting of him no matter what the outcome of his
personal struggle, but she always thought of him as a
heterosexual man who needed reassurance about his
masculinity. The right woman would fix him, she thought,
and perhaps a little therapy.

❦

Delia wanted very much to be that right woman. She invested
three years in an on-again/off-again romance — but she ultimately left Bryan. She felt angry. It took her a long time to realize that
she herself must face unresolved issues related to sexuality and
commitment before she would be ready for the relationship she so
desired.

Sometimes a prospective partner is unavailable not because he
is unwilling to make a commitment, but because he is unacceptable to you as a life mate. Some chronically single women find
themselves attracted by "bad boys." They are not unlike addicts in
their bravado. They do not see laws, let alone social norms, as
applying to them, and women may take a perverse pleasure in
their company — while at the same time feeling ashamed to be
seen with them.

Derek stood more than six feet tall; he had bulging
muscles and an ego to match. Even as he walked up to
the bar, Elise gave him her full attention. She liked his
wild, long hair, his silver earring, his tight blue jeans, his
leather boots, his demand for the bartender's immediate
attention. She moved to the stool next to Derek. Within
minutes, and without much preparation, she was taking
the seat next to him in his truck. He had a great and
urgent need for sexual attention, and he bluntly asked
Elise to relieve him. Later, she wondered why she had said
yes. In the weeks that followed Elise assuaged her guilt
and her pain with the thought that she hadn't really given

herself to Derek; she had just done the guy a favor.

❧

On some level Elise really knew she had been had — but that did not stop her from responding again to Derek's need when he asked for phone sex. Overwhelmed by feelings of degradation, she at last determined not to repeat her mother's lifelong history of relationships with abusive men — and she asked for help.

It is not always a man's flaws or weaknesses or attitudes that make him unavailable; often the chronically single woman is herself not ready for a mature relationship — her unconscious reason for becoming involved with an unavailable man in the first place. But the chronically single woman can sometimes be stymied simply by circumstance.

A man may be geographically unavailable to her, even for courtship, unless she is willing to move. With some men a difference in faith is a barrier unless the woman is willing to convert. And some men do not want children, a state of affairs that makes them ineligible unless the woman is willing to forego motherhood. In these instances a woman has little chance of deluding herself; she has a choice to make. But there is one potential impediment to marriage that a woman may not easily adapt to: children from a prior relationship.

When she first met Harry, Cheryl was pleased by what he said about his six-year-old son, Tommy; he seemed to be a good father and so, to her mind, a good candidate for a serious relationship. During their first two dates, as she came to know Harry, Cheryl liked him more and more. Unfortunately, though understandably, the dates had to end early, in time for Harry to take over from the baby-sitter. Cheryl didn't mind. She did mind somewhat that Harry's attention seemed to drift toward Tommy early in the evening, but she saw his concern as another sign of his maturity.

For their third date, Cheryl and Harry decided to

include Tommy and planned an evening he would enjoy: hamburgers and miniature golf. Fantasies of the readymade family began to fill Cheryl, and they felt good. Dates three through seven were all much the same. Of course Tommy liked being the center of attention, and all was well.

After five dates in a row largely devoted to Tommy, Cheryl was tiring of "the family thing"; she wanted more time alone with Harry. Harry, in fact, wanted more time alone with Cheryl as well — but, as before, his attention would drift toward home and Tommy, and the dates were sometimes unsatisfying. Then Tommy began to feel resentful that his father was off on a date with Cheryl or that, if they were all three together, he was not the absolute center of attention. As the tension in the situation escalated, there seemed to be no solution, and in fact there was none. As a veteran father, Harry was accustomed to setting aside some of his needs; Cheryl was not.

❀

Though it is not impossible, it is extremely difficult for someone unaccustomed to the many demands of parenthood to step into a readymade family. In Cheryl's life, Harry was the last in a long line of unavailable men; in another woman's life, Harry may very well be Mr. Right. Cheryl eventually chose to move on and seek a mate with whom she could start a family of her own. She left with a great deal of respect and love for Harry and Tommy; she had learned from them a lot about intimacy.

No doubt many women have found happy, productive, committed relationships with men just like the ones described in this chapter. But beware. If you find yourself attracted to a man who has some trait that limits his availability for a committed, intimate relationship, it is worth exploring why you want to spend time with a man who lessens, rather than strengthens, your chances of marriage. And if you have a pattern of relationships with such men, it is especially important to consider whether you have some ulterior motive for choosing such a difficult path.

# 4

# *Being Preoccupied*

Any woman who longs to be married is saving an inner space for her man. While waiting and looking, she may fill the space with some substitute for the man she hopes for in order to ease the pain of her loneliness.

Unavailable partners or some other person, place or a thing can be called on to the fill the space, as already described. "Temporary fillings" are self-defeating if prolonged, but they can be of value. One may, for example, fill the space with an enjoyable activity and, in the activity, find fulfillment. It is not unusual for people to meet a mate while doing what they enjoy. One may also fill the space with a temporary mate, and the relationship may be a valuable preparation or an enrichment.

In some cases, however, the temporary solution becomes a part of the problem, because the woman may compensate so well that she appears to be unavailable. She may *want* to find her mate; she may look for him high and low. But when men have the opportunity to get close to her, they get the impression she is already taken. It is as if a lighted sign over her head reads "Occupied."

Sometimes the sign may be lighted purposely to deter unwanted attention. In a nightclub, for example, a quick reversal of a cocktail ring seems practical, and at a party it's easy to say one's involved. But sometimes a man the woman would like to meet will see the ring or overhear, and then turn elsewhere.

Often these easy maneuvers are adopted by women who are afraid of hurt feelings — or any feelings at all. Polite lies are concocted to escape them, but lies are more likely to hurt than the truth. A simple "No, thank you" is entirely tolerable to a man who has self-esteem. And an offensive man will be spared further self-delusion by being told of his offense. It is especially important to remember that a woman owes no explanation for refusing a man's advances — and a less than honest answer may well start a rumor that she is unavailable.

It is not necessary for a woman to take a particular action to turn on the Occupied light: it is likely to go on automatically when a woman enters a temporary relationship with an unavailable partner. Even when she recognizes the relationship as temporary, and intends to keep her eyes open for someone better suited to her needs, she may become content enough, or busy enough, for the sign to light up. All relationships, even undesirable ones, require work, and her absorption may distract a woman from her goal and give others the impression she is occupied. Very often women learn that they cannot find a mate until they let go of a temporary partner.

For many chronically single women the Occupied sign may be permanently lighted, whether or not they are seeing other men. They seem unable to attract male attention and will have to find out what it is that has lighted that sign. Most begin to discover self-defeating behavior as they explore what it is they are occupied with.

Perhaps she is occupied by an addiction or a compulsion — by a substance, such as alcohol or drugs, or by a behavior, such as eating, gambling, working, or having sex. Addictions and compulsions turn on the Occupied light because the substance or behavior increasingly becomes the center of the woman's life. It is her best friend, her lover, her comfort. And she usually hangs onto it, for-saking all others.

> At one time Veronica accepted invitations to girls' night out and enjoyed the company of her office friends as well as the attention of some of the men at the bar. These days, however, she declined these invitations, and most others, anxious to get home by herself. There she could eat to her heart's content.
>
> Her compulsive eating usually started in the early afternoon after a modest and disappointing lunch with co-workers. Her thoughts would drift first toward securing some special treat she could secretly consume in the lounge. She would tell herself she'd make up for the treat with a diet dinner. By midafternoon her thoughts would move inevitably to that cherished evening at home with all she could eat close at hand. Socializing no longer held charm. Neither, really, did her evening of binging. Veronica could go through a meal for four in only a few minutes, not slightly distracted by the TV. Nor did she really enjoy her meal. She just kept eating until she got sick. No matter how it tasted, the food must be eaten.

❀

Initially Veronica did not recognize her bulimia. She felt and saw only her loneliness, thinking always how long it had been since she had been on a date. She blamed her social isolation on her 20-pound weight gain — a completely inadequate explanation, since she was a strikingly beautiful woman even when overweight. Once she was able to acknowledge her eating disorder and begin to examine its cause, the "Occupied" sign seemed magically to disap-pear. Suddenly, without losing a pound, she was attracting male attention as much as before.

This positive male attention stirred up a curious mixture of feel-ings in Veronica — fear, anger, and an overwhelming sex drive, in addition to the excitement she expected to feel. At first Veronica related these feelings to her extremely controlling mother, to her struggle to find an acceptable expression for anger. Later she began to explore the impact of her passive father, who so often brought his emotional needs to his daughters instead of his wife. Using her mouth to express herself rather than stuffing it with food was a slow, but ultimately effective, process. And it was her willingness to face her feelings, to explore their roots, and to express them verbally, instead of acting them out in eating, that made all the difference in Veronica's life.

When chronically single women are overweight, they often blame this one factor for their failures with men. True, physical appearance plays a significant role in first impressions, but it does not have the power we often invest in it. Personal and clinical experience suggest that often it is the obsession with food, much more than the extra pounds, that isolates the overweight woman. And this is usually compounded by a poor self-image — an excessively negative body image and a negative view of herself as compulsive.

Whether a woman is obsessive about food or alcohol, or something else, compulsions and addictions do tend to act as a deterrent to healthy relationships. Chemical dependency, because of its powerful mind-altering effects, is an especially powerful deterrent to healthy relationships. Potential mates are turned off not only by the addiction itself and its untold effects on appearance and behavior, but even more by the chaotic lifestyle it induces. Addictions and compulsions must be faced, and often professional help is required: their wellsprings are complex. They may stem from physical as well as psychological problems and may be serving a complex of purposes, as well as the purpose of filling a space. Once released from their tyranny, however, a woman can be available as never before.

Addictions and compulsions are only two of the preoccupations of chronically single women. The Occupied light can also be turned on by lost love, by carrying a torch — and the problem can be exacerbated by a tendency in some women to idealize the lost love. In a selective memory he may become the perfect listener, provider, lover, and companion — a man whose place no other can fill.

Annette and Bill met in college, where both were studying to become teachers. They were in their first year of graduate school when Bill's cancer was diagnosed. He would never complete his education; he would be dead within three years. Annette would always remember him as a teacher, however, because she had learned so much from him. She could talk for hours about his zest for life, his free spirit, and his emotional depth. When she thought of him, she always pictured him hiking with her in Sycamore Canyon with the sun on his face, the wind ruffling his hair.

She accepted invitations from admirers and somewhat enjoyed a dinner date or a movie with them. But eventually Annette would invite the men to go hiking in the canyon — with an always disappointing result. The trips were a test, and a test that most men would fail. These men might be handsome and nice and bright, but none was her Bill. None knew what it was to be dying and hiking in the canyon — and some didn't even enjoy it. Missing the intensity of those last years with Bill, she readily saw other men as shallow.

Finally George came along and refused to go hiking in Sycamore Canyon. She saw his insistence on sailing and snorkeling instead as an effort to control the agenda; she was blind to his wish that she share his interests for she was focused on Bill. In truth, George was attracted to Annette and wanted to create a history of their own.

Although it was difficult for her, Annette had to look not only at Bill at the height of their romance and in the crisis of his diagnosis but also at Bill in his illness. That wonderful brown hair was lost to chemotherapy and radiation. That free spirit collapsed when he moved back in with his mother to be close to the clinic. And his zest for life was ultimately quieted to a readiness for death.

Annette ultimately became ready to work through her feelings about Bill and his illness and death, which she finally accepted.

She said her belated goodbyes — and gave George a chance.

Sometimes a woman hangs onto a lost love not because she wants to keep loving him but because she wants to keep hating him — and in this way too she is preoccupied. For whatever reason he has left her, she feels betrayed, and she is resentful. Feeding that resentment seems to redress her sense of injury and somehow to fill up the empty space. She not only lights the "Occupied" sign but also repels men and women alike with her anger. She may extend her resentment to include all males.

> Miranda and Doug had been married for only a few months when he had his first affair. It was the first of many, but Miranda knew nothing about them until eight years later, when Doug's most recently discarded mistress decided to blow the whistle. She spared Miranda no details of his liaison with her and of others before that she knew of. Miranda had no choice but to believe. Her entire life with Doug now seemed a lie: their sex life, their spiritual life, their talk of the future. It all meant nothing now in the shadow of this shocking news. She dwelt on his deceitfulness.
>
> Four years later, divorced and alone for half that time, Miranda sat in a coffee shop with some girls from the office. For the sixth or seventh time they attempted to interest her in a blind date. Miranda was annoyed — in her church, she said, divorce precluded remarriage. But it wasn't just her church that kept her single. Men, she had decided, are never what they appear to be.

❀

Miranda had, at one time, chosen married life for herself. She could have chosen to work things out with Doug, for he had begun treatment to get at the root of his Don Juan behavior and was asking Miranda to join him at the counselor's office. She chose not to do so, but rather to divorce. She could have dated other men. She chose not to do so, but rather to distrust them. She fills her lonely inner space with resentment toward Doug, and she takes no responsibility for her choices. She chose to marry her resentment, and, so far, she has been faithful.

For a chronically single woman, unrequited love can turn on the Occupied sign. She may well have worked out in her imagination every detail of her courtship by this man she always wanted, never got, and cannot let go of. Any new candidate is immediately compared with him and found wanting, for imaginary lovers are, of course, perfect in every detail; they never cause disappointment or pain, only fulfillment. As in the fairy tales we grew up with, imagined stories end with living happily ever after.

From the moment their eyes first met, Phyllis knew this would be the man she would marry. His dark eyes looked so deeply into her that she imagined words would not be necessary. She had not dated since the death of her first love, and she was relieved that this man would not require explanations. He would just know. He would know that it was time for Phyllis to start dating again. He would know where to take her and when to take her hand. He would know when to take her. It helped that he was of a suitable age, and a colleague and a church member — but these were only incidental factors. After a full year, new dresses and other ploys had failed to attract him, but they did attract other men, and some asked for dates. One man, Frank, was genuinely appreciative of Phyllis.

He liked her, and he saw her new dresses as a sign she was ready again for romance. He was eager to take part — to share himself and to know her. But after three dates there was no denying she was comparing him with the ideal, imaginary lover who spoke truths with his eyes in Phyllis' fantasies. Frank was, of course, disappointing. He didn't even have dark eyes.

※

It took Phyllis a long time to realize that she was in love with her imaginings. Her recovery required letting go — of the mysterious man she would never know, and ultimately of her first love. This freed her to move on.

The lives of some women are dominated by a love for their fathers. Beyond feeling the natural love most women feel for a father, some carry a torch. They see a perfection in their fathers no other men match, let alone surpass. The lives of others are dominated by their fathers for different reasons, which often stem from the absence of a mother. They may idealize their fathers early on and trade in their childhood needs for his.

> Beth was only four years old when her mother died in a car accident, which also claimed the life of her baby brother. For Beth, in her mid-twenties, her mother was a distant shadow. But that shadow was overlaid by the image of mother's face in the photograph her father kept on the piano. Beth knew her father had been devastated by her mother's death; he had taken to drink, but after a few years, with the help of friends, he had settled down.
>
> Beth's father had become a model citizen; he worked to support the household and save money for Beth's college education. Beth, for her part, began early learning how to keep house and to cook; she enjoyed preparing meals for the two of them, and, in her pleasure, she sometimes wondered what her father would do without her.
>
> Beth's competence was also evident at school, and she received a partial scholarship to college. Instead of going away, she decided to stay on with her dad and attend the local community college, with a view, she said, to meeting a local man with whom she could settle down.

❧

With her self-esteem at a low ebb, she sought help. In exploring the loss of her mother, Beth reclaimed her role as a daughter, and in so doing let go of her role as caretaker; she also broke through her perception of herself as a wife. She was free to find a man for herself — and she found one out of town.

There are also women who are occupied by a childlike dependency on their parents, never having become individuals. Clinging to their parents, they are often unaware they are filling the space that is designed for a mate. Or they may be so dependent on their parents' approval that they are not free to choose a mate without it.

At the age of forty-two Maggie feared her ship had sailed without her. Twenty years earlier she had chosen Bob for her mate, a construction worker unacceptable to her millionaire parents. His struggle to work his way through college did not impress them, nor did his initiative and his love for their daughter. Nor did it matter that Maggie's happiness did not require millions. It was the family album that mattered to them, and, dependent on their approval, Maggie chose to preserve her page in that dusty book.

Maggie's efforts to find someone they could all love proved frustrating. The men she found interesting were unacceptable, and the men her father brought home from the office were boring. She met David at a company picnic, and he was a lot of fun. They discovered that their fathers worked together. It was an afternoon of many happy discoveries. Later Maggie discovered her father had not brought David home because he was Jewish.

❀

Maggie and David proceeded to date, and moved quickly into intimate waters. Everything seemed to come easily between them; their relationship was fluid. The fears which did come up for her did not stop her this time; she just shared them with David, who accepted them without question. David had issues to work on, too, and was very understanding. Maggie could sense that ship circling in her harbor again. A second chance. This time, happily, she did not wait for a consensus. Despite her fears, she got on.

Fortunately, by this time, Maggie was prepared to place her need to be married above her need for her parents approval. As is so often the case, the blessing of Maggie's parents came belatedly, when they saw that the marriage was happy. Well intended but unwise, they had forgotten an adult woman must make her own choices.

Some chronically single women have children from earlier marriages and find that these children light the Occupied sign. Without question, children properly occupy a great space in the lives of loving parents, but some single women are so enmeshed with their children that they become the victim of a manipulative child or of one allowed too much dependence.

> Stevie's father had died before Stevie was born, and the baby became the center of Judy's life. She stayed at home with him when he was little, and when her husband's life insurance was gone, she decided to develop a home-based business in order to be with her son. She began taking in other children and soon was operating a small day-care center. In Stevie's eyes, this was bad enough — having to share Mommy with five other kids. But then, when Stevie was four, Sam came along. He was a widower who came to call for his daughter — and then stayed for coffee. Stevie saw the writing on the wall when Sam stayed for dinner, and he had a tantrum. When his mother was dating he threw more tantrums. Judy was held hostage by her child.

❊

Unable to see Stevie as a *part* of her life, Judy saw the issue as a false either/or, either Stevie or Sam. So entangled was she with Stevie that she was unable to see his need to be disentangled from her — to be helped toward individuation. Nor could she even see Sam as a salutary father figure for Stevie. Because of Judy's preoccupation, no one's needs were met — neither hers nor Stevie's nor Sam's.

And Stevie was set up as the four-year-old man of the house.

Only a few of the most common things that can turn on the Occupied light have been discussed. Usually, of course, the light is turned on by an emotional preoccupation, but it may also be turned on by completely unconscious habits.

> Stephanie worked in a predominantly male
> environment; she was a biochemist in a research
> laboratory and the only woman within miles. Not that
> she couldn't withstand competition. Her black hair glowed,
> as did her green eyes. The men talked about Stephanie's
> eyes, and were interested in this new colleague as a
> woman who seemed to be soft and hard and bright and
> naive all at once. She saw it as a sign of respect when
> they addressed her as Mrs. Jordan. And she never
> corrected them.

❈

Stephanie was somewhat preoccupied by her work — but she would have responded warmly to an overture from almost any of these nice men. But they assumed she was unavailable. There was a formality about Stephanie that caused men to keep a respectful distance. In this case some scientific observation and simple reasoning led Stephanie — who became Stephanie, not Mrs. Jordan — to the solution: lowering her guard.

Women who are preoccupied are not necessarily deprived of male attention. Preoccupied women can be particularly attractive to chronically single men, who recognize them unconsciously as unavailable and so likely to say no to a commitment. When women begin to recover, most of these men will vanish. Some, however, have recognized the preoccupied woman as wounded, like themselves, and are willing to wrestle with issues of intimacy. Whether with the help of a man or a therapist or alone, the issues must be dealt with if the space is to be open for the right man.

# 5

# *The Revolving Door*

Not all chronically single women are chronically lonely. Some have no trouble meeting men and getting relationships started: they have trouble keeping them going. Some have been married and divorced, and may have had several marriages. Whatever the case, these women are very busy dating, mating, and leaving men, or dating, mating, and being left. Outsiders may see their lives as an enviable whirlwind of romances or as a pitiable series of failures. Their close friends see their despair — trapped, as they are, in the revolving door.

A teenager, of course, can be madly in love with Tom on one day, and with Dick on the next. These transitions may come with a lot of tears, especially if the girl was dropped. Despite the tears, girls usually adjust quickly — as soon as they set their sights on someone new.

It is not so easy as we mature, and it shouldn't be. For grown women attachments are more deeply rooted, and uprooting them can wreak havoc.

Some women seem to glide smoothly along from one

love affair to another — looking calm, well-adjusted, on top of it all. In fact they are desperate, hoping at each turn of the revolving door to find respite and the calm they appear to have. But they are afraid of attachment. Their losses are superficial because their attachments are too slight and unrewarding.

> Richard appealed to Jeanine because he was tall and good looking and a good dancer. Several of Jeanine's lovers had been satisfied — even delighted — with an affair with this social butterfly, but Richard was looking for something different. From the start he made a point of saying he was looking for a relationship, not an affair. The notion of "settling down" began to seem healthy to Jeanine, and even appealing. She encouraged Richard wholeheartedly and so did her parents.
>
> Joy abounded among family and friends, but it was short-lived. One month was about it for Jeanine. Richard was talking about their future, but she wanted *tonight* on the town; Richard was thinking of children, but she wanted *tonight* to have sex. "We're not getting younger," he said — and that was the end. She dumped him for a man who could do a better samba.

❊

Jeanine was bored out of her skull. Although she initially liked Richard, and had fully intended to pursue a serious relationship with him, she lost interest as the excitement of early courtship phased out. She wants to marry, but has never met a stable man who didn't feel like a paperweight. Jeanine's only long-term attachment, beyond superficial attachments to her biological family, is to her cat. She is a social butterfly, and in her eyes, men eventually just look like a net. The fact that her family was pushing their marital agenda on her provoked her resistance. Her recovery would require working on increasing the depth of her attachment to others, exploring the nature of her ambivalence, and detaching herself from her family's agenda.

Just as Jeanine failed to form any real attachment with boyfriends, looking to them only for entertainment, other women fail because they seek only admiration and constant attention. Such a woman can get downright high on early courtship, for male attention is almost like a drug for her. When the attention of early courtship fades, the erstwhile admirer is abruptly cast aside.

This time, Adrienne was sure she had found Mr. Right. Marv was everything she'd ever wanted: handsome, rich, and so very sensitive to her needs. He was so attentive: he opened doors and brought flowers, and he called her earlier than promised because he just couldn't wait to talk to her again. Mostly, though, Adrienne liked the way he sat and gazed at her admiringly for the longest time. Clearly, he was falling in love with her.

One month later, Adrienne began to wonder. Although he was still nice to her, she was no longer the focus of his constant attention. He had resumed most of his normal activities. Although he still called her almost every night, sometimes he called only to say, "I'm beat; I'm going to bed. I just wanted to tell you that I love you."

Another month elapsed before the explosion that ended their relationship. They had made plans to see a movie and go out to dinner on a Friday night. On Tuesday of that week, Marv called Adrienne to say that his boss had asked him to take over a Friday meeting with an out-of-town executive. Since he saw the request as a compliment and career opportunity, he accepted without hesitation, assuming he and Adrienne could renegotiate their plans. Not so. She reacted to the news using the foulest language she could think of and hung up on him.

Adrienne shook him off like dust from a rug. When Friday came, she dressed to the hilt and went out by herself. There she won the undivided attention of a well-dressed businessman, drinking alone at the bar. He was everything she had ever wanted: handsome, rich, and so very attentive. This time, Adrienne knew she had found Mr. Right.

❧

Adrienne had already been involved in more affairs than she cared to count. Although she had occasionally been rejected by an admirer after a brief involvement, most of her affairs ended abruptly when she exploded over some failure on the man's part to meet her excessive need for attention. Although she appears to fall in love easily, what Adrienne really loves is the undivided attention of men. She doesn't get to know them, and she goes elsewhere for a supplier as soon as they fail to come up with her "fix." Whether or not they are suitable candidates is anybody's guess.

Neither Jeanine nor Adrienne can succeed in relationships with men until they become more available for attachment. Jeanine, more aware of her ambivalence about attachment, has had an easier time exploring her mixed feelings. Adrienne, less insightful about her problems with attachment, began to make progress by reminiscing about her mother's aloofness, and the pain associated with these memories motivated her to seek attachment. For both these women, relationships formed with other women who have similar problems have proved to be an excellent starting place.

Some women, though able to form attachments, have such unrealistic expectations that they reject entirely appropriate and desirable partners repeatedly. Their ideals, being flawless are impossible to fulfill. Sometimes the nature of a woman's expectations provides a clue to the underlying issues at work.

> Marilyn had always known exactly what qualities she was looking for in a man, and Ken seemed to have most of them: her father's heart, Gandhi's social conscience, Alan Alda's sensitivity to feminism, John Wayne's grit, and Mel Gibson's eyes; if possible Mel's body would be nice, too. They met at a rally for a political action committee and recognized each other as soulmates.
>
> Marilyn and Ken had a natural rapport; all areas of

their lives seemed to fit. They had achieved a stable
relationship when Ken came down with the flu, and he
stayed in Marilyn's apartment. Flu or no flu, fever or no
fever, the whining was incomprehensible to Marilyn. How
could a man who had marched in the street against injus-
tice become a wimp in the face of a bug?

❀

The behavior that disgusted Marilyn so thoroughly is actually
fairly normal. While it would be healthier for men to acknowledge
their vulnerability consistently, it is common for them to save up
vulnerable emotions and express them *en masse* when they are ill.
Even the mightiest Wall Street warrior may revert to a fetal position
when nursing a cold or flu.

When Marilyn saw the little boy inside the man, it really turned
her off. As soon as he was back on his feet, he was out the door.
She could not tolerate weakness of any kind, not in herself and certainly not in others. The issue behind Marilyn's unrealistic expectations was her avoidance of vulnerability. Marilyn had identified
with her strong, silent father who failed to meet her childhood
needs. Unable to "beat" him (in the contest of conflicting needs), she
joined him. Recovery for Marilyn required reclaiming those long-
buried needs and working them through.

One form of unrealistic expectation that keeps women in the
revolving door is the expectation of conflict-free romance. Many
television shows and movies encourage this expectation; children's
books and fairy tales, too, carry the happy message. In real life,
however, an apparently nonconflictual relationship is patently
unreal. It is either dead or a lie. When children are somehow shield-
ed by their parents from conflict, they have neither a real knowledge of relationships nor the experience and skills to carry them
through.

Chrissy grew up in a family in which the illusion of
bliss was maintained at all costs. She was the youngest of

four children, young enough to be parented by siblings as well as parents. She was the little darling; everything she did was cute. The family album overflowed with pictures of precious little Chrissy. Although there must have been some sibling jealousy, it was never expressed. Chris got nothing but praise from this apparently loving family.

Now 50 years old, and no longer so cute, Chris was recovering from her third divorce. All three marriages ended due to "irreconcilable differences." Her first husband had returned to his old church, and Chris had interpreted this move as abandonment. Two affairs followed before her second marriage, which ended when her then husband confronted her about her credit card abuse. More affairs followed, leading to her third marriage, which ended when he insisted on having a weekly "boy's night out."

❦

Chris had come to view men as selfish and incapable of meeting her needs. When she sought help, she was about to give up hope of ever finding a man who could love her as her family had. In counseling she was encouraged to give up the expectation that her needs would always come first. She was barely aware that others had needs, and she was stunned at the prospect of conflict. She was, however, aware of the anger she had felt toward her husbands, and she learned to view it as a cue to negotiation, not departure. Her fourth marriage stuck.

Chris ran from conflict she was unaccustomed to, as she might run from an encounter with a strange man on a dark night, but some women avoid conflict because they know it all too well. And their fear leads them to repress their anger.

For as long as she could remember, Wendy had hated to make even a fuss. She prided herself on being a good sport and did everything in her means to avoid conflict.

As a child she put up with her mother's rage and her brother's teasing; as a teenager she gave in to her boyfriend's demand for sex. And as she grew older, she gave up more and more of herself as she accommodated to the multiple social, emotional, and sexual needs of her boyfriends. Nevertheless, they all left her within six months.

❋

These men had been seeking a partner with whom they could share their feelings, not an object on which they could vent their anger. They felt burdened by the power she had bestowed on them, by her dependence on them, and they were not happy.

After so many failures Wendy felt inadequate as a woman. She sought help to fulfill her desire to be a better partner, never sensing it was her very compliance that caused her boyfriends to move on. Eventually she began to acknowledge her anger and its repression, to explore her mother's fierce temper and her helplessness as its victim in her childhood. Soon she understood her fear of losing control of her pent-up rage and her terror of retaliation.

Mock confrontations with her mother and her boyfriends defused the explosive situations. Wendy learned gradually to stand up for herself, and even sometimes express her anger. No longer withholding, she began to connect and to make a new life.

At the opposite extreme from Wendy's compliance pattern of behavior is a control pattern. Whereas the compliant woman is perpetuating her childhood efforts to placate the controlling, angry parent, the controlling woman is seeking a remedy for her damaged self-esteem. And her frank abuse of power can create a revolving door frequented by men who appear to need fixing.

Deanna had a strength about her that many people had admired over the years — and some had used. She had always been relied on by her bosses and by her friends to work late, to help out in any emergency. They sought her out as the one most likely to make the best of a bad situation with the result that Deanna saw herself more and more in that light and began to volunteer.

By young adulthood, Deanna's pattern of involvement with fixer-uppers was well-established. Guys with potential, in Deanna's eyes. Surely, she thought, with her help the security guard, Fred, could become a policeman and the dilettante painter, a commercial success — but she was wrong. Most recently there had been Phil, an alcoholic, and again she had failed.

❧

In therapy Deanna saw she was choosing inadequate men and trying to rescue them, just as she had tried to save her father from the oppression of her angry mother. He had depended on her, and she was seduced by the power she had obtained; these men, however, had resented her control and moved on. Now tired of being the strong one, Deanna allows her vulnerability to soften her strength — and attracts a much stronger man.

Often it is a fear of emotional intimacy that causes a woman to bail out of a relationship, or set up a chain of events to cause a man to leave her. For though the thought of closeness may be appealing, the immediate prospect may be frightening.

Though it had not been easy for Tracie, at twenty-six she had become fairly skilled at starting relationships. She had learned how to flirt and how to become acquainted quickly; she had developed sound instincts in choosing partners and had enjoyed two longterm relationships with entirely eligible bachelors.

Her instincts did not fail her when she met George at an employee picnic. They were both hovering around the punch bowl, feeling a little on edge when George initiated a conversation by saying that frankly he felt awkward, not knowing just what was expected at an affair of this sort. Tracie was supportive. He appreciated her attentiveness and asked her for a date; he wanted to get to know her better.

The shop-talk of the first date gave way to more personal conversation, and their interest in one another became more serious. It was not surprising that George was stunned when he met the barrier reef. The odd boundaries imposed by Tracie had him baffled: she refused to acknowledge their romance to office friends, and after making love, she would never stay the night.

Tracie was not baffled for she had hidden behind the barrier reef many times before — each time the thought of being open had made her skin crawl. It was an unpleasant feeling, and she knew, despite her denial, it was the cause of her losing George.

❀

Once Tracie had broken through her denial to take an honest look at her defenses, she could see that she was still afraid her mother would smother her. Her commitment to honesty forced Tracie to find another way to set boundaries, flexible ones that allowed her to enjoy closer relationships with friends and loved ones.

Just as fear of emotional intimacy can prompt a woman to flight, so also can fear of sex. The sources of such fears may not be clear.

Beverly wondered often what had happened to her. She remembered her adolescent sexuality with wonderment. It had been many years since she had enjoyed spontaneous sex, and it was no longer easy to capture the attention of men. "I'm fat," she would say, "and that's why I'm single." Eventually her attention shifted to the more interesting question — why she was fat.

❀

Unlike most women who are seriously overweight, Beverly had not always had a tendency to overeat; it had begun in her young adult years when she left home, when her whole body suddenly seemed to scream at the world, "Stay Away!"

Ultimately Beverly traced her panic to her older brother's seduction of her at the age of twelve. In her journey of recovery, she was able to see her adolescent promiscuity as the result of her need to act out her feelings of guilt and shame, and not as the ultimate joy. She confronted, at last, the guilty one, the guilty brother, whose abuse had held her in thrall all those years. She was free of the need to stuff her mouth with food and free to rediscover her sexuality. Letting go of overeating involved opening her mouth, not to eat, but to talk to her brother. This was not popular with her family; some refused to speak to her. But her freedom was worth it.

Although her brother never admitted what he had done, Beverly derived benefit from having said it aloud. Never again could he torture her in her dreams; she no longer had to carry the shame. She was able to let his shame be his business and get on with her life. While she will be dealing with the many dysfunctional aspects of her childhood family for some time to come, Beverly's confrontation of her brother freed her to re-discover her sexuality, and ultimately to embrace it, as a precious gift. She no longer needs to keep men at bay.

Sometimes a woman who is able to establish and enjoy good relationships with men is nevertheless caught in the revolving door because of fear of commitment. Like her commitment-phobic male counterpart, she may attract partners who are also afraid of commitment and unconsciously choose her as "safe." She may also attract men who have poor self-esteem and are determined to bolster their self-image by wrestling a commitment from her.

Penny wondered whether she would ever meet the right guy. At forty-four, although she had met many wonderful men, Penny had been involved in only two relationships that had lasted longer than six months. Each of these had lasted a few torturous years, as the men tortured her with their efforts to force a commitment and she tortured herself with her efforts to make a decision. In both cases, the men finally moved on. When she felt relieved, Penny figured she had done well to not marry them.

It was five months into Penny's relationship with Ted, and she could feel the pressure building. He had already begun talking vaguely about his hopes for his future, and it wouldn't be long before he would begin to add her to the picture. She tried to recapture the tender feelings she had been enjoying, but then she would perceive Ted as a needy, demanding baby she would like to leave on someone's doorstep. The more aloof she became, the more demanding he was of reassurance — and the battle was joined.

Unwilling to again suffer the tortures of pressure, Penny stepped back and studied her own resistance, later asking why Ted needed so much assurance. When Ted proved unwilling to examine and take responsibility for his needs, she stopped resisting and made a free and independent decision to part with him — and later to choose men who were not needy and insecure.

# 6

# Ambivalence

Of all the forms of self-defeating behavior chronically single women fall into, those stemming from ambivalence are the hardest to recognize and resolve. A common example — one many women have to work out — is the conflict between the need for a relationship and the need for safety. It is normal to want and need both; however, in order to take the personal risks necessary to form relationships, the need for safety and the desire for companionship must be reconciled. Reconciliation begins with our awareness of our conflicting needs. Ambivalence is an internal conflict between two seemingly incompatible emotions or needs, acting on you at the same time. It is common to have a mixture of feelings about people, places, and things, although you may not be aware of just how mixed your feelings are.

A conflict between two equally strong emotions or needs may be difficult to resolve, because one or both may be driven by unconscious forces. A woman may be aware, for example, of her wish for companionship but not in touch with her fears about the risk involved. Her progress will probably be slow and frustrating until her deeper fears come to the surface, where they can be addressed.

A common source of ambivalence about relationships is fear of intimacy. Sometimes the symptoms of anxiety are on the surface, obvious to all: the sweaty palm when you hold his hand, the voice that cracks when you try to express your feelings, the mind that goes blank, the giggles. When the fears are unconscious, however, they can create a very different look.

> Betty and Frank met at a church-sponsored lecture for single professionals over thirty. On that evening, a therapist was scheduled to speak about "How To Have A Healthy Relationship." At the end of the talk, when they met, both were determined to follow the suggested plan of action and reap the rewards. Frank had taken voluminous notes on the "rules of engagement," and their first conversation focused largely on these.
>
> Their early dates consisted of meeting at church functions and going for coffee later. They spent a lot of time talking. They did occasionally go out and have some fun, but they were making a concerted effort to stay with serious conversation, trying to comply with the rules. "Avoid physical contact at the beginning," was a precept. Betty and Frank shared their ideas and some personal stories, but very little of themselves. They shared no feelings or passion; they were following the rules.

❀

On the surface, both Betty and Frank appear to be totally dedicated to the development of a healthy, intimate relationship. Their membership in a singles club, their attendance at the lecture, and their obvious efforts to follow the advice of the speaker all seem to indicate a desire for a healthy, intimate relationship. Each was, however, playing the role of student as a defense against intimacy, and their relationship soon died.

The role came easily to Betty, who always had been a good little girl, who did everything by the book. Following rules had been rewarded by her critical parents, but this time, she saw that following rules didn't work. Her anger at the oppression of the rules at last emerged, and she shed the lifetime role of the good girl to make room for the complex identity that had been stifled for so long.

Repressed anger is often the source of ambivalence. Some women harbor a deep resentment against men, not overtly apparent in their behavior but all too clearly apparent in their faces. Such women, when confronted by themselves or someone else with their resentment, will have a ready answer, for they have surely been mistreated. But then, who is paying for the maltreatment? The victim.

> Caroline had come to this singles party with three girlfriends, and she had been looking forward to it. Now she was sitting alone, watching the crowd. Her girlfriends were all in the company of men, either talking or dancing, and Caroline wondered why she was alone: "I'm a nice person," she thought. "I want to dance. I just don't get it."
>
> She stirred her drink and studied her girlfriends. Not prettier than she, and not better dancers. She took note of the sexy behavior of one, and she was writing it off as pandering when a fine looking man came her way. She cracked a smile — and on he went. That smile did seem like a mere crack in her hardened face. And the man kept walking.

❀

Caroline was aware she was angry with men — and for good reason. She had been left at the altar in her youth, then divorced, and recently raped. Clearly, her anger and pain would need to be addressed. Still she worked very hard at keeping these feelings under control. Everything involving men seemed *unfair* to her, however, and that was the clue to the childhood origins of her anger.

Caroline eventually explored her childhood experience and found there the source of what was in fact a deep-seated prejudice. She had been imbued with the bitterness of her grandmother, irremediably subjected by the mores of the times to her husband's verbal abuse — and the bitterness of her mother, too, who advised Caroline to choose wisely ". . . because you will be stuck with them until you die."

Only when Caroline was able to identify the family legacy of resentment could she give men a chance.

Sexual identity confusion is an obvious roadblock for the woman who wants marriage, but the cause of its persistence can be obscure. It sometimes stems from an inner sense of betrayal and sometimes from shame. Even when a woman has decided that she wants to be in a heterosexual relationship, the presence of homosexual yearnings may prevent her from making such progress, and she may also be deterred by repressed memories.

> Eileen did not question her sexual identity until her late twenties. Her confusion started just after her mother's death, when a girlfriend came by with flowers and comfort. The friend was as surprised as Eileen when the friendly comfort became stimulating for them both and more than friendly comfort followed. The incident was disturbing to Eileen, but not grossly upsetting, secure as she was then in her heterosexual identity. The incident was repeated, however, with another friend when Eileen was again in pain, and this time it led to a two-year affair. It was terminated suddenly by Eileen, in the bedroom, when a wave of rage and then nausea confused and frightened her.
>
> Eileen had to explore the meaning of those horrible feelings and sensations. Efforts to re-visit that last encounter brought more waves of nausea and rage, and eventually memories surfaced which helped fill in some of the blanks. Eileen was only four years old when her beloved maternal grandmother began to molest her. It had

started with bathtub play that got progressively out of hand, and progressed to frequent enemas that had no wholesome purpose. Although Eileen lived with her parents, Granny was the primary caregiver until early schoolage years, when she died. With Granny's death, Eileen's memory died too — or at least went into suspended animation, until another woman's loving touch triggered these horrible memories.

❀

Since then, over a period of four years, Eileen has not been involved in a significant relationship; her female lover made all women repellent, but she has not dated men. As she was approaching forty and was anxious to have children, she sought help, hoping to uncover whatever obstacles stood between her and marriage.

Recovering memories of abuse did not instantly solve Eileen's confusion about her sexual identity, but it allowed her to shed the veil of shame that had kept her from close relationships for so long, and it thus opened the door to a sexual life.

Many women who have no question about their heterosexuality are nevertheless ambivalent about men, whose occasionally crude behavior they find offensive. Such a woman may want a man's companionship and sexual attention but, at the same time, dread day-to-day life with the offender.

Kelly's earliest complaints about Alan involved his talking with his mouth full. He didn't do it often, but Kelly was troubled enough to mention it to friends. As their young courtship progressed, she noticed other aspects of his eating habits which also bothered her. After a few months, when he really felt comfortable, Alan's table manners deteriorated even further and on occasion he would cough and spit. Kelly wondered "Why do men do this? Women *never* spit."

Nevertheless, their relationship continued, and

eventually they became sexually intimate. Alan snored. It was the last straw. After spending two consecutive nights trying to sleep on the living room sofa, Kelly asked Alan to go home and stay home. End of the affair!

❀

Though most men are not so crude as Alan, they may have habits and behaviors that put off women. Though an assertive woman can negotiate some consideration with regard to manners, no negotiation can ward off snoring. Some women have a hypersensitivity to these offensive sounds, suggesting an earlier trauma.

For Kelly, all offending male behavior was intolerable, for she associated it with her step-father, whose gross crudity had seemed to rule her childhood. A "bullish, arrogant pig," he had dominated all family dinners with his tall tales and crude behavior, while the rest of the family echoed mom's silence. At the age of eighteen, Kelly moved out.

Until her encounter with Alan, Kelly had been unwilling to deal with her feelings about the offensive behavior of her partners and had repeatedly moved out — into one relationship after another. Having faced her anger with her mother and step-father, and the sense of shame that always colored her relationships, Kelly is now free to enjoy a much greater sense of intimacy. Today she is not only able to confront offensive men, she is also attracting more refined partners.

For some women ambivalence about marriage stems as much from professional or social concerns as from personal ones. Perhaps her career or her sheer enjoyment of the single life will cause a woman to question the appropriateness of marriage in her life. She will probably remain frustrated until she can decide between marriage and the single life. Marriage is not for everyone.

Since the days of "Dr. Kildare" and "Ben Casey" Mae had known her life's ambition: to be a physician. In her teenage years she dreamed of healing sick babies in The

Peace Corps; in her college years, the fantasy faded. She was thinking now of a small private practice, though fantasies of being "The Love Boat" doctor did cross her mind. In medical school she was too busy to indulge in much fantasy, and after a grueling internship, accepted a residency in internal medicine. Then on to a clinical position on the staff of the local hospital, with a view to debt reduction, and, hopefully, marriage.

Four years later Mae had advanced in her career and was responsible for a considerable amount of teaching and supervision in addition to her own patient-related duties. Though she was frequently asked out for dates by her associates, Mae was reluctant to cross over professional boundaries, and on weekends she was busy preparing lectures.

Mae was not so concerned about her empty social life as she was about her fatigue, for though she enjoyed her professional life, she found it draining. It was clear she had to establish a life outside her work to fill her emotional and spiritual needs.

❀

Most careers can be arranged to accommodate family life and other purely personal needs if the career-minded woman is determined to have both. Mae, however, was not determined. She saw the contrast between her vital work and the too-quiet joys of home; so she remained ambivalent. Not until she became depressed and sought intervention could she break the lock.

Ambivalence can spring from an unquestioned primary loyalty to parents, fed by the comfort of their automatic approval. A powerful family bond can work almost unconsciously to preclude other wishes. Even a conscious thought of starting a family of one's own may feel like betrayal. This perceived betrayal is avoided, and marriage remains an unfulfilled dream.

No one understood why Sue played hard to get, nor did she. She was average in appearance — no knock-out, that's for sure; one would think she would do well to encourage some of the men who came her way. Sue didn't encourage anybody. She might occasionally accept a date if her interest in the man was substantial or he had offered an appealing invitation. She often insisted on meeting at a restaurant or some other public place before giving him her address or phone number. Sue did not make it easy.

It seemed Vern might be an exception, for she had known him a long time and liked him very much. With unaccustomed enthusiasm she accepted his invitation to an art show — more enthusiasm than she might have mustered had she not tried and failed to get tickets herself.

Then, a few days before the opening, Sue's mother stopped at her apartment with a surprise: she had obtained tickets for the whole family — for dad and herself and for Sue and her brother. Sue did not hesitate to accept the invitation to join the family party, without a thought of Vern. When she casually broke their date the next day, with an allusion to her family, she was surprised and even aghast at his show of anger.

❀

It did not occur to Sue to tell her mother she had a date, or even to suggest they make a party, to include both Vern and her brother's girlfriend. Sue was too deeply buried in the family forest to see the trees, and she may well remain there until lightning strikes.

Occasionally a woman's ambivalence about marriage stems from coupling it in her mind with motherhood, which she is loath to undertake. Sometimes, fully aware of the choice she would make, she is ashamed to admit it. "We are supposed to want babies," a patient recently told me, "and women who don't are freaks. Something is wrong with me."

Norma began mothering when she was a small child. She was the oldest of six children and helped her mother bring up the younger five. Although there was a father "in the home," he wasn't there much, between working, drinking, and gambling. Norma's mother, though a home-maker, was not fully present either. She was immature — more like another child for Norma to care for.

As the first-born daughter of this sad, depressed woman who was herself the child of an alcoholic, Norma had thrust upon her not only the care of her siblings but also the responsibility of helping her mother to function. In fact, during most of Norma's adolescence, it was more like helping her mother stay alive, because her depression caused her to consider suicide frequently. Norma had taken charge of her pills more than once.

Thanks to Norma, all had survived, and now, at thirty-five she had a clear road before her. Her younger siblings were on their own, most married, and her mother, who had received treatment and divorced Norma's father, was enjoying an active social life. Everyone had a settled life but Norma, and she needed a new definition — a focus — for her life.

While Norma did feel a longing for her own child, she had for too long experienced the burdens of motherhood and wanted to enjoy her freedom. Finally, she worked through her resentment, and decided she wanted to experience her new freedom in a marriage without children. It was amazing how quickly her social life picked up.

For some women ambivalence may have its roots in fantasy. They tragically embrace solitude for the purpose of calling forth the caring and comfort of the man of their dreams.

Kathryn had anticipated this moment, and she wanted to make it meaningful. It was the moment of Dan's departure. After several weeks of struggling with the future of their relationship, this weekend Kathryn and Dan had agreed to separate. And now, early on a foggy Monday morning, the moment had come to carry out their decision.

Their actual goodbye was rather plain. But as the front door closed behind Dan, Kathryn moved to the sliding glass door. There she watched his descent down the poolside stairs, his movement across the deck to his car, and his hesitation once seated behind the wheel. Then the slow progress of his car through a fog; it created only the slightest disturbance in the cloudy mist. These details would be etched in her brain.

One lone tear presented itself, lingered a moment, and slowly began to trickle down Kathryn's warm cheek. There she was, in her dark blue velour robe, with her angora cat beside her, her hands wrapped around a cup of cinnamon tea. Kathryn watched her reflection in the glass. What a wonderful commercial, she thought, for this soothing tea, and regretted no one was there to film it. She lingered as long as she could, until the trickle tickled, and the cat demanded attention.

As long as she could remember, Kathryn had lived her life for the imaginary man who would see and chronicle her tragic life, and he would always be caring. In childhood she pictured him as a knight, trapped in an armor rusted by the tears he had shed over her. He was a powerless knight, whose tears caused him to be tightly trapped in his rusting armor.

Kathryn's knight, and the cameraman, were fantasy fathers, but their tears and recognition of her pain could not assuage her deprivation. It was too late for that. Long ago there had been too many nights when her father had come home to find his little girl in tears as her wild-eyed mother abused her. He had stood by, mutely uninvolved.

Kathryn's anger and pain finally broke through her world of illusion. She reached the stage where she was at last able to give the men in her life a real chance.

# Part Two

# UNDERLYING PROBLEMS

# 7

# *Issues With Father*

When a chronically single woman begins to look inside herself for the sources of her difficulties with men, the natural first stop is her relationship with her father, for it is with him that her first male/female relationship has been established. Even if she has never seen him, his impact on her psyche is profound; in this case, it is his absence, rather than the nature of his presence, that is primary in shaping her way of relating to men. If he is present, his day-to-day affect and behavior will shape her attitude toward men, her perception of men's attitudes toward her, and her perception of herself in relation to men.

It is through her father's eyes, also, that a little girl forms her image of a woman's value. If her father places a high value on his relationship with his wife and treats her as a cherished partner, the little girl's self-esteem will be well grounded. If he values his wife as a cherished possession only, her self-esteem will be hollow. If he belittles his wife, her self- esteem will be damaged. And if he is domineering or passive she will not see marriage as a partnership.

Often, however, the father's attitude toward his wife is not clear-cut. He may value her as a maid, for example, but resent having to deal with her emotional needs — and this father's daughter will learn to seek men's attention by offering her services. Or a father may appear to value his wife as a partner but gawk lustfully at the woman next door; so his daughter, not being fooled, will rely on sex for being valued. Many variations are possible, and the chronically single woman must explore them, and her father's relationships with other women as well, if she is to see how he has shaped her.

As Jungian analyst Linda Leonard has observed, the father, as the first man in his daughter's young life, will shape not only her relationships with men but also her relationship with the masculine side of herself. It is his role to break her infantile bond with her mother and to be her bridge to the outside world. As Leonard observes, because he is male, he is especially "other"; in his masculinity, he is different from herself and her mother and, therefore, will influence her uniqueness and individuality. He will shape her attitudes toward work and success in most cases. And, as Leonard observes, it is he, traditionally, who provides her ideals. He is, moreover, her model in the spheres of authority, order, decisiveness, responsibility, discipline, and rational thought. So it will be if the father is fully and appropriately effective in his role. Needless to say, that is seldom the case.

Sometimes a father intrudes inappropriately instead of fostering his daughter's development, but more often a father's faults are "sins of omission." In either case, each woman formulates her own image of the ideal father. Some women paste the face of the fantasy father over the face of the real father, denying his true nature and enjoying a lovely relationship with a man who does not exist. Or a woman may see her father realistically but measure him against her ideal rather than against the norm.

A mental health professional might write the following description of the ideal father:

The ideal father is a man who actively participates in
the life of his daughter. He loves and respects his wife and
demonstrates a healthy, positive attitude toward women.
He has a special place in his life for his daughter, which
does not disrupt, but perhaps enhances, his marriage, as
father and mother share the experience of parenting. He is
a mature individual who can model responsibility,
decisiveness, and initiative through his productivity at
work and his involvement in the community. He enables
his daughter to find and foster these attributes in herself
and also encourages, through his appreciation, the emergence of her own unique talents and traits.

❀

A more immediate, and perhaps more effective, description was
expressed by a three-and-a-half year old girl:

Daddy's are to fix boo-boos. My Daddy is a good Daddy.
When I have a boo-boo, he kisses it "All better!" And then
he lets me sit in his lap until the boo-boo goes away.

❀

When a chronically single woman describes the ideal father, however, the texture changes:

He would never leave me, but he would allow me to
leave him. He would tell me generously of all the things he
loves and values about me and would be careful in this
criticism. His love would be obvious and abundant and
wholesome. He would be proud of me and tell me so often;
his everyday conduct would make me proud of him.

❀

Of the many life events that can disturb a woman's sense of connection to her father, the total loss of him is most devastating.
Whether he died, or abandoned the family, or perhaps never knew

of his daughter's birth, his absence will have a profound affect on her life.

The family photo album had always given Trudy the impression that her father was ideal. He was handsome, athletic, and had a kindness about his face that made you want to know him. The pictures of him with his family revealed a man in awe of his baby daughter and very much in love with his wife. But Trudy never knew that man, except in her fantasies, for when she was only 18 months old, her father was struck down by a brain hemorrhage and sustained permanent damage. He would return from the hospital occasionally, but these episodes were usually brief, and his need for further medical care would inevitably take him back.

As she got older she had to help her mother with some of her dad's physical care, which traumatized her and made her feel relieved when he left. Trudy also had to deal with the neighbor children's jokes about her father's drooling or shouting out gibberish. In time, Trudy began to joke about him, too; in this way, she at least had some sense of bonding with the other kids. There was no one else: no brothers or sisters, and a mother who was totally consumed with a job.

Now thirty-two, divorced, and recently separated from a boyfriend, Trudy entered therapy with a real trepidation; she doubted whether she could ever have a healthy relationship. She'd been married to an alcoholic after a long line of relationships with damaged, needy men. "Are all men like this?" she often wondered. Trudy thought she might have found an exception in her most recent boyfriend. He was ten years younger than she; nevertheless she thought he had real strength. Unfortunately, it was not deep strength, but a cocky attitude. He was damaged, too.

As Trudy began to examine her history with men, it was easy to see how her relationships had taken shape. As a girl, wanting her father's attention like any other little girl, Trudy was put in a caretaking role with her father. Her earliest memories of her father involve being the little helper as Mommy bathed her husband's damaged body, changed his adult diapers, and tried to feed him pureed foods. She would notice, with curiosity and disappointment, his lifeless genitals. The guilt she felt about her reactions to his body gave seed to the self-doubt that would later cause her to question whether she deserved a healthy relationship.

Trudy was also influenced by the loss of her mother's emotional support. For all intents and purposes, her mother had died in the same accident that took her father away. Trudy's mother, who may not have won awards for emotional availability before the accident, survived her husband's disability by turning off her emotions. She functioned on auto pilot. She was a model of amazon strength for her daughter, fertilizing the seeds of caretaking planted so early.

What made the seed flower, however, came later in childhood, when Trudy joined with the neighborhood kids in making fun of her father. The guilt and pain she suffered, in having to sacrifice what little remained of her relationship with her father in order to have friends, was beyond words. Her shame in betraying her father was enormous. Trudy's guilt drove her to the side of damaged men, where she would unconsciously seek to atone for her "wrongs."

Trudy's recovery requires facing that shame, and all the pain beneath it. She has had to examine not only who this man was — an invalid, not a valid father — but also the nature of her reactions to the shell that once housed a loving father. Her willingness to face these feelings will lead to forgiveness — of the father who could not recover, of the mother who did her best, of the neighborhood children who giggled at something strange, and ultimately of herself, the lonely little girl who really loved and missed her Daddy. Then Trudy will no longer need to care for damaged men.

The origin of the self-defeating behavior of many chronically single women lies in some form of abandonment by their fathers. Very often the abandonment is physical, through desertion or death, but the child also feels abandoned if her father is emotionally out of reach.

Little Beatrice had always loved her Daddy; she was his baby, and she deserved his special attention, so she felt, because she was there — when her mother had gone off to work and her older brother to his books. Little Bea would tug at his leg as he sat watching the TV screen, and he would eventually pick her up, set her on his lap, and tell her about the program. She knew his attention was really on the program and so would wait eagerly for the commercials, when he would be all hers.

By the time she was in grade school, he had become completely engrossed in his TV programs, which he clearly preferred to a child's idle chatter. And sometimes he would express annoyance at her efforts to get his attention. Still, Beatrice would stay by his side, often sitting on the floor in front of Daddy's sofa, and she would try to interest herself in Daddy's program.

By the time Bea was in high school the family had a new house, and Daddy had a den, to which he withdrew every night. She often walked to the door in the hope of a sign he wanted company, but she didn't intrude, except to bring his dinner. By the time Bea was seventeen, she was spending her evenings with friends.

These friends with whom Bea spent her evenings — and her nights — had become legion by the time she was thirty-seven — and she had done many self-degrading things to win their attention. She had become an alcoholic, and, in recovery, was extremely disappointed to learn that sobriety did not fix her troubles with men. She wanted a healthy relationship. She had given up seeking the attention of casual partners, who had always cast her aside. But now she was faring no better with men in recovery who had little time for her; though more gently, they also cast her aside.

❀

These men were busy in a more productive way than Bea's father had been, but she was nevertheless just as neglected — revealing Bea's pattern of trying to *win* a man's attention. She had become almost compulsive about the challenge, successively trying to win attention by being cute, by being responsible, and by being sexy. Most recently, she had tried instead to demand it. Yet it eluded her.

At last Bea saw that her father had, in fact, not cared, and her anger surfaced. Beyond it was the realization that no efforts or demands would elicit genuine attention from an uncaring person — and that a caring man would care. She found one.

Some fathers who are not essentially unavailable, who are able to care, are nevertheless emotionally unavailable to their children, and to others as well, because they are so involved with their wives, defined, in a way, by marriage. Meanwhile, the daughter starves.

> In many ways, Clara came from an ideal family, and she had been told so many times. Her father was an attorney, specializing in family law; he often volunteered his services through the local legal aid office. Her mother was a child psychologist, often treating families her husband referred to her; they seemed ideally suited to parenthood, given their interest in children and families. They were also a popular couple, and active in their church and in civic affairs. But although everybody seemed to like Clara's parents, no one knew them very well, she observed, and she felt that way herself.
>
> Clara's first memories of her parents, when she was small, were very clear; they were always sitting at the dining room table, which was awash with books, and shuffling papers and writing things. They didn't notice her, though she saw them clearly. They were involved with each other, and she would crawl beneath the table with her doll and watch their toes as they entwined. Sometimes she would suck her dolly's foot and fall asleep, trying to connect with this vision of love.

As Clara grew older and stayed up later, she watched her parents cuddling, and she would try to cuddle too, curling up at their feet to watch television. She was never discouraged; they seemed to welcome her efforts to connect with them, but they did not reach out to her.

There was little conflict in Clara's home, and only one argument she could remember, over her college education, about which she had not been consulted. Her father was gung-ho for education and her mother for social adjustment — an argument that resulted in the squaring-off of an Ivy League college against the state university. They were astonished by Clara's suggestion that she attend the community college and live at home. Her mother won — but it didn't matter.

At thirty, Clara was lonely, discouraged, and exhausted from her efforts to connect with others. Although there had been occasional exceptions, most of Clara's boyfriends had been passive and reluctant to make a commitment to her. Whether with girlfriends or dates, Clara found herself repeatedly taking sole responsibility for initiating and sustaining relationships. She was very skilled at getting attention, but the intensity of her needs scared friends and dates alike, and they disappeared.

❀

Although Clara worked hard to form satisfying relationships, something always got in the way; it was mostly her unmet needs, but it was also her shame about being so needy. She might say she was just looking for friendship, or perhaps romance, but in truth she was looking for the love that parents provide. She wanted someone to adopt her.

Early recovery for Clara involved being more honest about her needs, and facing how separate and acutely lonely she was because of her parents closeness. A turning point came when, in her imagination, she was able to crawl once again under that big table and feel her loneliness. She was then able to begin to grieve and to put her childhood longings behind her.

Some daughters are left wanting more by inadequate fathers. Sometimes fathers disappoint their daughters because they are simply not very smart, and sometimes because they are socially inept; unhappily they fail to provide a bridge to the outside world. Sometimes they are disappointing because of a characterological passivity.

No one ever knew for sure what was wrong with Reva's mother. Some said it was early menopause, and one neighbor suggested that perhaps she was possessed; whatever the cause, she was one angry woman, and the whole town knew it. One could seldom walk by the house without hearing Reva's mother yelling at somebody. Sometimes it was Reva, and sometimes her older sister, but it was usually Reva's father. In her mother's eyes, he could do nothing right — and she told him so with great regularity.

The greatest pain in Reva's life was the memory of her father's silent suffering. He never stood up to his wife — not to help his daughters, and certainly not to help himself. Tolerating her abuse, he seemed, with every onslaught, to move further and further away. In little Reva's mind, her mother's anger was killing her father and taking him away. She wished she could help him, but she did not let herself wish that he could help her.

Thirty-five years after leaving her family home, Reva recognized herself as an expert on passive men. She had married and divorced three and dated countless more. She had always been attracted to "nice guys" who turned out to be depressed, and wounded passive men. Reva would adopt them; she would hear their sad tales and encourage them in improving their lives. They did nothing, of course. So failing tenderness, she tried the scourge. And when tongue-lashings failed, she left them.

Several previous attempts to work on her problem had

done little to help Reva. She had some insight into her identification with her mother, who also had become enraged with a powerless man. But she had so far not yet seen her identification with her father and her compassion for him as another victim. Soon she was able to see herself as powerless to help her dad, and at last to see his failure to respond to her own silent suffering and her silent screams for help. Her pain and anger were enormous.

❧

Before finally achieving her goals, Reva had a brief relationship with a man who was more like her mother than her father; he was abusive. A troubling relationship it had been, but it had given her the opportunity to exercise some of her newfound power, for she was able to do in this abusive relationship what her father had not been able to do — to say no, to say stop, and to leave. The next man she dated is the one she married — a man able to use, not abuse, his power.

A different dynamic is at work when the father suffers from an addiction or a compulsion. Though he may wish to be available to his wife and daughter, his addiction or compulsion will displace them at the center of his life. And if he is addicted to a mind-altering substance, such as alcohol or a narcotic, he may well be not only emotionally unavailable but also abusive.

Lisa's childhood home was a happy one. Lisa's father was happy: a pretty wife, a decent job, good friends, and three loving children. Lisa was happy too; she liked that her Daddy carried her on his shoulders, wrestled with her on the livingroom floor, and cuddled with her on the sofa in front of the TV.

Lisa was the oldest, the only girl, and the closest to Daddy. She noticed everything about him. When he began to take a boy's night out, and came home looking happy but smelling of beer, she approved. Later, when he started going out by himself, she worried about him. And she missed him. But it was when he started drinking at home that she knew there was a serious problem. There was lots of evidence: he was aloof, even unapproachable; he was moody; he fought with his wife over bills, over his drinking, and over any little thing; he was getting thin, except for a swollen abdomen. He didn't look like her Daddy anymore.

Lisa changed, too. Once an outgoing, loving child, she was becoming a withdrawn, depressed, and tense little girl. Efforts to reach out to her father gave way to efforts to stay out of his way. When his drinking escalated to the point of violence, however, Lisa went into hiding. At twenty-nine Lisa had a well-established history of relationships with abusive men. She had obtained restraining orders against two of them, but she had never successfully terminated a relationship; she had left many times, but she had always come back. The men had left her.

🌼

Clearly, Lisa's attachment to abusive men stemmed in large part from her feeling of guilt. She felt guilty about being her father's favorite and about being unable to help him regain sobriety. Having experienced him sober, she was unable to accept him as the abusive drunk he had become. To unravel her identification with the victim role, Lisa had to examine the many roles she had played in her dysfunctional family. To her brothers, she was scapegoat; they blamed her for their father's abuse of them. To her mother, she was rival; she had stolen much of her husband's affection. To her father, she was almost a mascot — a symbol of the best of his healthier days. In reality, Lisa was a lost child, not really known by or connected to any family member.

Her recovery required not only embracing these realities but also coming to terms with her powerlessness over her father's alcoholism. Her guilt began to fade as she examined the nature of her relationship with her father and explored the impact of her mother's passivity in the face of his abuse. While there is still much work ahead of her, Lisa has been able to turn away from abusive men. She is definitely on the road to recovery.

When an addiction or a compulsion takes hold of a father, his daughter is inevitably damaged in some way: even what are sometimes called benign compulsions are not benign. And workaholism is a prevalent one.

> Dana's parents loved her very much. Since there were many demands on their time, they engaged a live-in housekeeper, Maria, when she was four, to establish continuity of care and to make sure her needs were met. Her mother, not a working woman, was sometimes at home in the afternoon, but most often she was away, involved in some civic or social event. Maria was, in fact, a most loving woman; she was also an excellent cook and liked to bake special treats.
> Dana's father, a real estate developer, started every day for her with a good-morning kiss as he was leaving, slightly rushed because of commuter traffic. She could still smell his aftershave lotion and the leather of his briefcase. Maria, often smelling of cinnamon, prepared breakfast, and afterward Dana woke her mother with a forehead kiss as she left for school. Upon returning from school, Dana was greeted at the door by Maria, who had milk and cookies for her in the kitchen; if Mom was home, she was usually watching television. Then homework time, and then neighborhood play, until Maria called her for dinner. Mom was usually at home for dinner, and complaining about Dad's being late. Then it was TV time, and Mom usually retired alone to the TV in the master bedroom, rather than join Dana in the den. Sometimes Dana would stay out in the kitchen to help Maria with the dishes.
> Weekends were much the same, except, of course, that there was no school. Dad worked on Saturdays, and Mom often had social engagements. By her teenage years, however, Dana began to suspect that these "social

engagements" were an affair, and she turned all the more toward Maria, until later, when boys and parties consumed her attention.

Dana began her dating life with dramatic efforts to gain the attention of the most popular boys in school. And when she succeeded in gaining the attention of the high school quarterback, she built her social life around him. She was a cheerleader and homecoming queen, but also, to have a life of her own, she said, she became president of one of the service clubs.

After high school, Dana dropped the quarterback, finding that he wasn't all that bright. The dating career that followed was marked by a great ambivalence. Dana worked hard to gain men's attention, but was inevitably disappointed in them. At twenty-four she complained, "I don't understand men."

⁂

Dana's absentee father had left her with a lot of questions about men. He had left his wife and daughter to care for their own needs. Dana had watched her mother try and fail to build a satisfactory life for herself in the shadow of his demanding career, and had ultimately seen her seek out other male attention instead. In her own way, Dana had done much the same — but she had had no father to help build a bridge for her to the world of men. Only her mother was a model, a woman who had never fully emerged from her father's shadow.

Early in her recovery, recognizing her tendency to shadow men, Dana was inclined to blame her mother for her present difficulties. Later, she felt her anger toward her father. In the long run she realized that blame was not helpful, only the expression of her feelings. A full ventilation freed her to focus on the development and expression of her own identity — a journey that eventually led her into an exciting love affair.

As mentioned at the beginning of this chapter, some fathers, though depriving their daughters of the fatherly love they need, still leave these daughters wanting less from them, not more. And clearly the incestous father is one of these.

> Alice's childhood, as she remembered it, had been tortured: her mother had been mentally ill and her father, a disappointment. At seventeen she had married a sexually abusive husband who had raped and sodomized her repeatedly during their early marriage. Separated from him and planning to divorce, Alice, at twenty-six had become a compulsive overeater.
>
> Over a period of eight years, she started and discontinued therapy several times. During most of these years, she did not date anyone; she had two male friends, but one was gay and both functioned as brothers to her. Her concern was not her relational problems, but her eating disorder. Finally, shortly after her father's death, having achieved no real progress through her intermittent stabs at therapy, she expressed a willingness to make a serious investment in it. It was suggested she add some body work to her regimen, and through it, a very different childhood story emerged.
>
> Alice's father had viciously raped her on a regular basis, over a period of about two years, beginning around the age of six. She remembered clearly his taking her, late at night, from the room she shared with a sister to another room, where unspeakable things occurred. She remembered the rape, though a number of the details still elude her. She eventually remembered, also, being sexually molested at an even earlier age by a trusted neighbor.

❀

At first stunned, and then shattered and sleepless, Alice eventually touched her rage. She scrambled to express her emotions, and when they were verbalized, she began to heal. Today having learned to use her mouth to express herself instead of overeating, she is dating and happily slim.

Father/daughter incest does not always result in a long social drought such as Alice had endured. Many incest survivors have active social lives, though some act out their abuse, or their shame, in promiscuous behavior — reliving the "bad girl" role foisted on them in childhood or, perhaps, seeking control over what was once terrifying.

Many women identify strongly with incest survivors, but have no conscious memories of a sexual encounter with their fathers. Though some of these women later recall repressed memories of sexual abuse, others identify because their relationships with their fathers *felt* incestuous. Without sexual intercourse, and even without implicitly sexual contact, the basic dynamics of an incestuous relationship and consequent emotional trauma can be present.

Shawna was the firstborn of four girls and her father's best friend: though it wasn't so obvious in her early childhood, by the time she was twelve or so, it was obvious to all. Shawna and her father had a relationship that was the envy of her sisters and of her mother as well. No one understood Dad as she did, it seemed; he always sought her out when there was something on his mind. Sometimes it was problems at work and sometimes his concerns about her sisters; eventually it was problems in his marriage. He talked with Shawna not only about day-to-day marital troubles but also about sexual dysfunction, though usually spared her the details. "I hope you find someone more compatible," he said. "It's very frustrating to have a partner whose sexual needs are so different." Shawna felt vaguely that her mother was to blame for not meeting her father's needs, but she prayed he would never tell her exactly what that meant.

Shawna's father began to struggle with his feelings about losing his daughter. As she became increasingly popular, involved first with one and then another boyfriend, he felt threatened. He criticized her friends and found none of them even remotely adequate to be involved with his daughter. On the one hand, Shawna resented her father's dependency on her and wanted to make a life for herself. On the other hand, she felt responsible for him and wanted to protect him from the pain he appeared to be in.

At thirty-two, though she had lived on her own for many years, Shawna had never resolved this internal conflict, and, of course, she had not found anyone good enough to suit her father. She was seeking help with her ambivalence at the insistence of her most recent boyfriend, who, like her father and previous boyfriends, tended to get his way with Shawna. Fortunately, she very quickly saw this boyfriend's controlling, dependent nature. One day, she unexpectedly told him he was just like her father. He may have left in a huff, but she had finally arrived.

✦

Although several months passed before Shawna felt strong enough to confront her father, she was growing all along. After she did confront him, she was able to set limits on new boyfriends and withhold information from her father until she had determined her own opinion of a man. Her relationship with her mother, who still sees her as "the other woman," has not been resolved, but it has not prevented her from forming healthier, deeper relationships with women. The men she dates today are not dependent on her.

Another father that daughters want less of is the controlling father.

Peggy's father was the fourth of seven children born to poor farmers in the Midwest. Though both the oldest and the youngest child completed high school, the middle children were needed at home — the boys, to help their father with the work on the farm, and the girls, to assume the role of their mentally ill mother. Peggy's father, though a bright man, felt deprived and inferior because of his lack of education, and, even as a youth, dreamed of children to whom he would give a better chance. At his earliest opportunity, he selected a gutsy young woman, married her, and moved out west. He started out in a factory job, but pursued his talents as an inventor and eventually started his own company, with which he was very successful. Sadly, his feelings of inferiority were aggravated by his association with men who were better educated than he. More determined than ever to give his children a better chance, he focused relentlessly on their schoolwork. Report cards were examined and discussed in every detail. He focused most intensely on Peggy's performance. She was the oldest and therefore responsible for setting the pace, he thought. If her *A* average slipped only slightly, he restricted her limited social life even more. By her junior year in high school, he had nailed down her college career to his complete satisfaction. By the end of that year, Peggy had begun to question whether she even wanted to go to college. At the end of her senior year, one month after graduating, she eloped with her high school sweetheart, Ralph, who had often complained about how controlling he found her father. Ralph had plans of his own, and within six months, Peggy was pregnant with one of the those plans. Feeling controlled again, she left Ralph after the birth of their baby girl and went out to find herself.

For the next twenty years, Peggy focused on rearing her daughter and dated only occasionally. Then, faced with an empty nest, she was faced also with an absence of social contacts. She came to a workshop for single women wondering, "Are there any decent men out there?" and "Why do men always have to be in charge?"

❀

As Peggy worked out her resentments against her father and reclaimed the right to design her own life, she was surprised to realize how much power she had given away in her rebellion, how little identity she had managed to achieve. She learned in recovery that to rebel against domination is to be controlled by it.

By working through her resentments against her father, she has at last freed herself of his domination. No longer rebelling against it, she has transcended it. She has been able to open the door to education — in a field of her choosing — and now pursues a career as an artist. She is developing her identity through her work and also in her relationship with a man she has indeed chosen. She is a success, not of her father's making, but of her own.

# 8

# Issues With Mother

Before launching into a discussion of the mistakes and misadventures of mothers, it seems important to acknowledge that historically, women, as mothers, have received a disproportionate share of attention in psychological research relating to children. They have been blamed for everything maladaptive in their children's behavior, from thumb-sucking and bed-wetting to eating disorders, while the impact of the father's absence or faulty child-rearing practices has often been ignored. The disproportionate focus on mothers has been, in some measure at least, circumstantial, for the mother has been, traditionally, the principal caretaker for the child — and, as such, the parent more available for study. Perhaps, too, there has been a bias among male researchers.

Nevertheless, the impact of the mother on a child's life is major — and is particularly significant in the case of the chronically single woman, for first lessons about attachment occur in the womb. While researchers may still argue and explore the extent and nature of the cognitive processes of the human fetus, few would deny the presence of responsiveness to comfort and discomfort, attachment and alienation. It does, indeed, appear that the intrauterine environment is one of the first factors to influence human behavior — mother's love and attachment or ambivalence, along with her physical health.

Even more widely accepted is the impact of the birth process. In an effort to reduce the trauma, hospitals have developed birthing centers, providing special lighting, posturing, and music to ease the transition. Some have even experimented with birthing under water, again to ease the new baby's transition. Also, the newborn is often laid upon mother's chest, in the hope that hearing the familiar heart beat will help the baby feel more connected and less anxious.

Implicit in these efforts is the recognition of one of the mother's most vital roles in her daughter's life: to provide a sense of connection. For clearly, a strong bond between baby and mother is vital to the baby's survival and early development, and much of what a child knows of attachment is learned in the mother's arms. When a baby is held close and gazed on with love, a sense of attachment is the result, of trust and of love. But a baby merely slung on the hip of a mother whose attention is elsewhere is not likely to feel attached. In exploring issues of attachment, therefore, it is vital for the chronically single woman to examine her early relationship with her mother.

Beyond attachment, the heart of mother's role involves nurturing. Early, mothers nurture through physical care, and the quality of that nurturing is measured by its adequacy and its gentleness. Later, mothers nurture through their attention, encouraging development by supportive responses to trials and errors. Ultimately, like fathers, they nurture by encouraging autonomy, individuation, and separation by encouraging the child to have a self.

Because they are female, mothers are the primary role models of female children. They show their daughters what it is to be female — not only by how they treat them but also by how they treat themselves and other females, and in how they respond to the treatment others give them. It is not enough for a woman to be kind to her daughter. No matter how kind she may be, if she allows others to abuse her or her daughter, she is declaring that women are abusable. Nor is it enough for her to encourage her daughter's intellectual and social development. If she works outside the home but still does the lion's share of the housework, she is declaring a woman to be a household drudge. Since these messages are not explicit, it is important for a chronically single woman to explore the lessons she has been taught about being female. Mental health professionals often describe the ideal mother in terms of her fulfillment of these important roles:

> The ideal mother is the one who wants to be pregnant and who can reaffirm her desire even after the waves of morning sickness or the waves of agony in childbirth. She feels joy in having a daughter, reflecting her own self-esteem as a woman. Her attachment to her daughter is evident at birth, in close snuggling and abundant eye contact. She delights in signs of the girl's development and encourages her daughter in finding and expressing her talents. She treats herself and other women with dignity and kindness and tolerates no less from others. She is not intimidated by her daughter's growing independence and shows interest in her daughter's increasingly separate life.

❀

A three-and-a-half-year-old girl reflected another perspective in her description of the perfect mother:

> My Mommy fixes me toast when I get up . . . and she doesn't have to go to work, so she fixes lunch, too. She gives me lots of hugs and kisses. She takes care of everything. She lets me watch TV whenever I want.

❀

When chronically single women are questioned about the ideal mother, they tend to focus less on childhood images of mothering; their descriptions tend to reflect frustration with their adult mother/daughter relationships.

She would like me. She would like herself. She would
hardly ever criticize me. She would be proud of me. She
would be happy with her life and have interesting people
to share it with. She would not need me, but she would
enjoy my company. She would be there when I needed her,
but she would not be upset when I didn't.

❀

Mothers are human, of course, and often do not measure up to
these high ideals; some come closer than others. When the gap
between the ideal and the real is particularly wide, the daughter is
left wanting more from her mother — or at least, more mothering.
Sometimes women look for mothering from a man.

While many forms of abandonment or estrangement can create
a wish for more mothering, nowhere is it more apparent than in the
daughter who has lost her mother to death.

When her mother was diagnosed as having cancer,
Donna was only four years old. She had no way of
comprehending at that young age how her mother's illness
would devastate her childhood and her life. So far it had
been a happy childhood. Her parents, who ran a small
business together, were successful enough to hire plenty
of help. They took lots of time off to play with Donna and
her younger sister — camping, fishing, hiking, and
spending lots of lazy days at the beach.

By the age of seven, Donna was an expert on the
impact of cancer. After the first of a few rounds of
radiation and chemotherapy, she caught the first image of
her balding mother and noticed the loss of those soft,
brown tresses. She saw the wigs all in a row for her
mother to select from, and she knew their wiry feel. She
knew also the long waits for the doctor's call in the hope of
remission. Donna understood then, at the age of seven,
more about cancer than she did about baseball or
"Sesame Street," and she was also starting to understand

about cooking and folding laundry. She was mother's helper, and ultimately mother's substitute.

When she was ten, Donna began to understand about giving up. Her mother had relapsed for the third time and looked far too weak to fight yet another battle. At one time Donna might have volunteered to fight it for her, but she was, by then, tired too — though it would be many years before she could admit to it. She was weary of the struggle, and she wanted to have a mother, a real mother.

Donna's mother lingered for eighteen months before dying at home. Her death was quiet, as was the funeral that had so long ago been arranged for. Many wept, and several adults, in an effort to comfort Donna, encouraged her to cry. She just didn't feel like it.

During the next year Donna's family went through some major adjustments. Her father's business was growing again, and he engaged a housekeeper; Donna, at twelve, felt somewhat at sea, for she was used to carrying the housekeeping responsibilities herself. At the same time her father started dating, and remarried two years later. Though Donna liked the woman he had chosen, she didn't like having a step-mother; she didn't ask for much mothering. When the family moved to a different school district just as Donna started high school, her father arranged for counseling to help her with the adjustment, but Donna found the sessions boring and shortly quit.

Donna returned to therapy at the age of thirty-four complaining of fatigue. She was tired of needy men. Though she had had only two significant relationships during the past ten years, both had been with needy men who looked to her for strength and leadership. She was more than tired of the role, and not hopeful she could ever find another. She wanted to know where she could find a man like her: responsible, smart, and rational. (She meant *unemotional.*)

❀

In therapy, Donna walked out of at least half a dozen sessions in a huff when the conversation led too close to her pain about her lost childhood. She was terrified of her own neediness and became furious at any attempt to expose it. It was especially difficult for her to maintain her tough exterior around a nurturing female therapist.

When Donna finally gave up and let herself experience her pain, she was afraid it would never stop. She didn't want to need anyone for she had learned early in life that the people who are needed may get sick and die or go off to work and remarry. She also expected others to feel disdain for her needs just as she did — but when she was neither judged nor abandoned, she reaffirmed the trust that she had taken for granted in the earliest years of her life.

Donna had years of grieving to catch up with — for the mother she lost, the mothering she lost, and the childhood she lost. And there were many lessons to come before Donna was able to engage in an intimate relationship with a man, as she shed her amazon role and sought and came to know herself. She had to learn to make friends and to accept support, which she comfortably does now as a wife and mother.

Just as Donna was deprived of her mother's care in her childhood by illness and left wanting more, so is the daughter of an addictive or compulsive mother. As mentioned earlier, the deprivation is most acute in the case of a chemical dependency, which brings with it mind-altering effects.

> To this day, Zoe has never known her mother sober. In her infancy and early childhood, Zoe saw her mother only occasionally, having been remanded to her grandparents custody immediately after her birth, along with her older brother. She knew all too well from her grandmother that her parents had not even put up a fight to keep her. Then, suddenly, when Zoe was five, just before she started kindergarten, she was returned to this stranger-mother, and her stranger-father as well, cut off from the only parents she had known. Now, seemingly on a whim, she

and her brother were being returned, with no explanation or preparation; it was as if the herd was being moved back to the north pasture.

It was not a familiar pasture. Her mother drank daily to the point of intoxication. Almost every night, during Zoe's entire first year at home, there was a fight, as Zoe's father tried to stop her mother's drinking or they quarreled about something else. When the fighting stopped, as young as she was, Zoe knew this was somehow not a good sign; her father left. That he didn't take her and her brother with him broke her heart.

For most of the next seven years, Zoe's life was a nightmare. The child support payments her father sent were not enough to cover her mother's liquor bill, let alone rent and groceries, and she was too incapacitated to work. On an unsteady basis, rent money and food were somehow provided by grandparents and her mother's endless string of boyfriends. Though able to make friends, Zoe was so ashamed of her mother that she never invited them to her house and eventually came to turn down their invitations in order to avoid an expectation that she would reciprocate.

Shortly before Zoe's fourteenth birthday, a miracle happened: her father came to take his children to his home. Even faced with a change of school and the loss of her friends — and despite attachment to her very sick mother and despite a complete lack of warning — she welcomed her father as a returning hero. She expressed nothing but gratitude and claimed that she had always known he would come to her rescue. Never mind that she was totally uprooted for the third time in her life. Never mind that she would not see her mother again for several years. She was going home.

Zoe would remain grateful for many years — grateful for any attention that would come her way. The older she became, the less discriminating she became about the source of the attention; at twenty-eight she was dating almost any man who asked her and sleeping with many. The ones who wanted her, she found boring; the ones she wanted, found her insubstantial. She was like a dandelion: pretty, but easy to pluck and quick to wither.

&#x273F;

Zoe's greatest fear was that she would always be alone. She gave any man a chance, fearful that he might be the last man to ask. She had no basis even to hope that someone would come along who would love her and want to stay with her; she surely had no basis for trust. She had no idea she was lovable, for she learned in her childhood only that she was unlovable; she was completely lacking in healthy models of love and commitment.

Early in her recovery Zoe focused on her relationship with her alcoholic mother, and a lot of anger emerged as she began to examine the impact of her mother's daily drinking and serial boyfriends. She also felt some anger at the family system at large, which had failed to intervene in any meaningful way on her mother's behalf, or on hers and her brother's — giving them an illusion of attachment and love, and then casting them aside without warning. First her grandparents and then her father had deserted her.

It was more difficult for Zoe to discover her feelings about her father; she felt indebted to him and reluctant to find fault. When she did eventually recognize his selfishness in saving himself, and postponing for so long any fathering, she recognized also her anger and pain. Focusing again on her mother, but now with pain and a sense of loss, she was able to grieve — and so ultimately freed herself of her fear of attachment, her poor self-esteem and her pessimism about being loved.

In contrast to Zoe's mother, some mothers deprive their daughters of love and attachment because they are otherwise committed. Most often it is the career woman, competent in the extreme, whose interests are focused outside the family. But it is quite possible for a mother to be otherwise committed when she has no job, and even without appearing to leave the home.

Tess had always been as cute as could be and had a lot of pictures to prove it. Ribbons, bows, frilly dresses, and priceless expressions all told of a happy childhood. In many ways it seemed an ideal childhood for both Tess and her older sister. Her father, who worked as an engineer at a nearby plant, rarely worked overtime, placing a high value on his family life. Her mother had given up her career in teaching to be with her girls, Tess and Joan.

Her mother's plan worked well until Joan started school, and then it seemed a good idea to Mom to do volunteer work where Joan was enrolled. Tess went to preschool, feeling somewhat deserted, but she didn't mind much; it was fun. Then Mommy volunteered to be the Brownie Scout leader for Joan's troop and soon began setting up at-home activities for the older girls that Tess was too young to join in. Not only was she left out of the barbecues and sing-alongs; she had to share her bed with a foolish girl who was scared of cricket noises — and she was chastised for being selfish when she complained.

The following September, Tess started kindergarten at Joan's school where Mom still volunteered, and it was nice to walk home with her and Joan. That year she was sometimes allowed to join in when the Brownie's had fun. Mom, however, was expanding her scope, and that same year got involved with a youth group at church. Then came the deluge of youngsters who demanded her attention and care — her friendly ear, sometimes a meal, and sometimes shelter. Before long the den was made into a bedroom with twin beds, just in case — and it was amazing how often they were filled. Tess complained of this invasion once or twice, but was again chastised for her selfishness.

By the time Tess was in middle school, her mother had developed a latchkey program for strays, for anyone left alone after school. She played with the younger children on the livingroom floor, while three or four teenagers did their homework at the dining room table, enjoying Mom's snacks. As they left, usually before dinner, they would tell Tess how lucky she was to have such a loving mother. "Yeah," she would say, "Mom loves kids."

By the time she was in high school, Tess had developed sad eyes, and she had quit coming home after school; she visited friends' houses or went to the mall. Planning her future she applied to out-of-state colleges and was accepted by three. She chose the one farthest away, in California.

Twenty years later Tess was still in California, looking for Mr. Right among accountants and engineers and sometimes businessmen, all left-brain types. She would impress them with her degree in economics and tell them of her preference for an active, independent lifestyle; courtships would begin easily, and end in disaster. The trouble was that once Tess got close to a man, her neediness would overwhelm her, and then this seemingly confident, independent woman would find herself whining on the phone for attention. "Do you really like me?" repeated so many times, was more than they could take.

❀

Those men will never have any idea how much Tess was holding back; she had tried so hard, for so long, to keep her needs out of sight — for herself and for others. And often she gave herself the same verbal slap that had shut off her needs in her childhood: "You're just being selfish."

On the contrary, Tess was not selfish, and she was surely not self-absorbed. She had avoided introspection for so long that it was difficult for her, in recovery, to pay attention to her needs and feelings. Her early efforts to go inside and feel her needs was truly frightening, for she felt it was her need, her vulnerability, that had cost her parents' respect so long ago. She saw, however, that her mother had not been lost because of her need, but had not been there. Then, having grieved over her mother's loss and the needs that would never be met, she found those needs no longer so demanding. She became approachable, and she attracted a very different kind of man when she was no longer in heavy denial of her real needs.

A daughter may be confused about whether she wants more or less from a needy, baby mother who looks to her for the fulfillment of some of her needs. She leaves her daughter wanting her to be there less; at the same time this mother, so childishly focused on herself, leaves her daughter wanting more.

When Becky started therapy, she offered the history of an unwanted little girl, molested by her brother, ridiculed by her father, and seen by both parents as a burden. There was nothing this little girl could do to win the love of her family; no one was there for her. The family was poor in love, poor in spirit, and poor in the pocketbook. As the little girl grew, so did her pain; she was bright and increasingly able to see and understand her father's ridicule. Her mother offered no help. She was alone.

The story was most interesting because it was not about Becky. It was about Becky's mother, and it was almost inevitably foremost in Becky's mind because she had heard it so many times — sometimes to make her feel guilty for a frivolous request but most often to make her more aware of her mother's suffering. By the time Becky was a teenager, she had heard this story more times than she could count — along with her mother's running account of the more recent tragedies in her life, including her neglect by Becky's father. She continually demanded mothering from him, and at last she gave up and divorced him. Becky took up the job of mothering, fearing she would be divorced too.

After seven therapy sessions Becky's own story had still not come out, though almost every aspect of her mother's life was well known. Efforts to elicit personal history seemed only to frustrate her, and finally it became clear: Becky didn't have a story; Becky didn't have a life. That was her story.

At twenty-four Becky had been out on only a couple of dates, both arranged by friends. Though pretty, she had never attracted much attention. She did have a few girlfriends, but none very close. She had studied accounting and was working for a tax preparation service while studying for certification. Strictly businesslike, she never made connections with the people she met at work. She exchanged Christmas and birthday cards with her father, and that was that. Once a week Becky had dinner with her mother, and since she invariably had no news, she listened once again to her mother's story or her more current tales of woe. Who wouldn't seek help to find a way out of such a bleak existence?

❦

It was not easy to engage Becky in therapy. She was so used to living in response to her mother that the process of initiating a dialogue was completely foreign to her, and intimidating. There were many long silences. But finally Becky broke the silence, with sarcasm. "I think I'll start a Get A Life Foundation," she said, "and be the first poster child." She also found it amusing that her work called for her to balance books, when she seemed to have no knowledge of an asset column — only liabilities galore. She was angry, and she was bright — and these were the first clues of the identity to be discovered.

The road to that identity was long, winding, and full of obstacles, for she felt a tremendous guilt at the prospect of separating from her mother. It felt as if she were putting her up for adoption. After many weeks of struggling with her ambivalence, Becky reported a dream which suggested that the struggle was over. Becky was carrying a baby girl, who was thin and marked with scratches — some scabbed over, some bleeding. She wandered everywhere with this baby, seeking help but unable to speak. Her frustration mounted, and she finally screamed out, "Will somebody please help me?" When she screamed, a hospital appeared, and she entered. She then handed over the baby to nurses in an intensive care unit. And she left.

This dream marked a significant shift on two levels: if one sees the baby as Becky's mother, her struggle to have a life independent of her wounded mother was over and she could love her mother without carrying her; if one sees the baby as Becky's own wounded self, she was willing to trust a therapist to help her and could be sure that help would come if she would ask. A long period of grieving followed this dream, but with every passing week, Becky showed increasing signs of life, and although visits to her mother continued to stir up feelings of guilt and confusion, they no longer isolated her from others. Six months after she started therapy, a co-worker asked her for a datc — and she was on her way.

A daughter whose childhood needs have been neglected but who surely is not left feeling she wants more is one who has been sexually abused by her mother — the victim of mother/daughter incest.

> It was only by accident that Lizzy ended up getting help, for she did not think she needed it. At thirty-seven she had been involved with many, many men — a few long-term relationships and many brief affairs. On the rare Saturday night when she had no date, she and her best friend would go out to a nightclub, whcrc new friends would be made. Never a dull moment in this woman's life. Her best friend was not so content as she, however, and asked Lizzy to attend a Friday night workshop with her; since Lizzy thought "Chronically Single Women" was "real cute" and she had no plans, she agreed to go.
>
> Lizzy had a peculiar response to one of the guided imagery exercises designed to identify obstacles to intimacy; she complained of feeling ill and left early. On a follow-up call she explained she had not really been ill, but had felt trapped, and just needed to leave. As she talked about her feelings, an unusual story emerged.
>
> Though she had no words to describe it, Lizzy had

always known about her mother's anal fixation. Her
earliest memory was of lying across her mother's lap, face
down, laughing and relaxing until inspection began. Then
her mood changed. Lizzy's mother thought an inspection
very important, and sometimes called for an inspection
"just in case." Whenever Lizzy went potty, however, a
thorough and complete examination was made. Though
long in Lizzy's unconscious, her mother's fixation one day
sprang into her consciousness — when her mother, yet
again, expressed her delight in the Coppertone billboard —
the one with the doggie pulling off a little girl's swim
trunks and exposing her bottom. Lizzy was now too old for
the inspections, too shocked by mother's interest in other
girls' bottoms, and she set her realization aside.

In high school Lizzy's social life was normal; she was
popular and had lots of dates. When she became sexually
active in college, Lizzy had one affair after another. One of
her conquests, however, sensing her detachment and
hostility, expressed his anger at being objectified, and
said, "Are you trying to prove something?"

❀

Indeed, she was. Although there were many dynamics at work in
Lizzy's pattern of relating to men, that long-ago date had hit one
nail on the head: Lizzy had serious qualms about her sexuality.
Proving over and over again that she was desirable to men was very
important to her. For several years she even kept a list of men she
had slept with, wanting to make sure that the number of men never
fell below the number of years she had been alive. It was thus that
she measured her self-worth.

Like many survivors of mother/daughter sexual abuse, Lizzy was
a long time in therapy before she used the word incest to describe
her childhood experience. Sometimes she would just sit and stare,
holding her breath, fixing her eyes, and waiting — just as she had
apparently done during inspection. But the time for waiting had
passed. It was time for Lizzy to talk and to deal with her feelings.

She had avoided them because, though she had never felt any substantial attraction to other women, she had been afraid that she would discover she was lesbian if she talked about her mother's abuse. It was important to explore the impact of being sexualized so early in life by a woman, but in Lizzy's case, her preference for men was clear. She made a commitment to abstain from affairs, and the process of forming a more intimate relationship began. It was a long and difficult, but successful, journey.

Without violating sexual boundaries, many mothers create dynamics similar to these created by those who do, through their excessive need to control.

Early courtship was usually pleasant and smooth, but sooner or later, her man would want to do something "his way." Indeed, Shirley had a pattern of attracting men for whom control was important, and eventually it would show up in the way they handled money, negotiated dates, and conducted themselves sexually. Also Shirley sometimes construed behavior as controlling that was not so at all. Sensing her resistance and her anger, the men would sometimes withdraw, or sometimes she would.

When Shirley began to explore the roots of her issues with control, an interesting story emerged. She was the second of four girls, and clearly Mom's favorite. Their father lived at home, too, but was very passive, and not really involved in his daughters' lives. His passivity would be the subject of many, many marital fights — although his involvement in the fights was limited to listening and grinding his teeth. Little Shirley would watch these fights with a great deal of pain and anxiety. She was afraid that her dad might break loose someday and kill her mom.

To prevent such an unthinkable event, Shirley took on the job of keeping her mother happy. The survival of the family, she felt, depended somehow on her giving her mother whatever she wanted. As a youngster she gave up wearing the jeans she preferred, and wore the frilly dresses Mom had selected. As she grew older, it was in the choice of hair styles and boyfriends that Shirley acceded to her mother's wishes — and then her college major. Never did she continue to see a man of whom her mother disapproved. Then, when Shirley was twenty-six, her mother suddenly died in a car accident.

As the daughter closest to her mother, she stepped in to help her father with the funeral arrangements — he was completely devastated — and she made all the choices without difficulty. After the funeral, she stayed with her father for a short time to help him become adjusted. When a few weeks had passed, she returned to her own apartment, to get on with her life. She was happy to be back in her own place; her father was starting to get on her nerves.

In the year that followed, much of Shirley's life came under her control. She redecorated her apartment, bought many new clothes, bleached and cut her hair, and started a new job. Then she started the search for a mate, which was not so successful.

❀

After five years of frustration and disappointment, Shirley decided to explore her relationship history, and two issues related to control became immediately apparent. One was her tendency, since her mother's death, to select men like her mother, who wanted to control her choices and dominate their relationship. These men Shirley fought, resisting their control and asserting herself, as she had been unable to do with her mother; she was making up for lost time. The other was her tendency, in imitation of her mother, to assume the controlling role herself. With these men she tried to exert the power of which she had been deprived by her mother's control over her. This issue was harder to come to terms with, but her willingness to own her struggle with control, to be more curious about men and her reactions to them, made all the difference in Shirley's life. Her willingness to share power in a relationship made her a better partner and attracted better partners, and she married one.

Controlling mothers come in many varieties; they aren't all angry, and they aren't all domineering. Some want to be a daughter's best buddy.

Freda loved her mother and regarded her as her best friend. They did everything together — shopping, sampling restaurants, traveling. You name it. And Freda's mother was an excellent companion; she was bright, spontaneous, and a lot of fun.

When Freda was only ten years old, her father died of a heart attack, leaving his young wife alone. Since he left his wife and daughter well provided for, Freda's mother was able to carry out her wish to stay at home, to be there for Freda during her developmental years. When Freda graduated from high school, mother and daughter entered college together.

In the years that followed, both Freda and her mother dated quite a lot; both were interested in getting married. A couple of times, they even double-dated.

That all changed when Freda met Jack, who immediately meant much more to her than a pleasant date. She liked everything about him — his dimples, his thoughtful papers on literature, his quick responses to the instructor's challenges. He was exactly the kind of man Freda was looking for. It was mutual. Jack asked her to go out after the second class. Freda's mother liked Jack too. She was supportive of the budding romance, and she was so pleased by Freda's choice that she often made arrangements for her and her date to join the young couple. Freda was disgusted by Jack's increasing attempts to avoid these double dates. She was stymied when he refused to have her mother and her date come along on a weekend trip he had planned for him and Freda, alone.

Wanting not to hurt her mother's feelings, Freda suggested other arrangements — perhaps a one-day trip that would include her mother and her date. Not recognizing and honoring the bonding Jack was offering her, she hurt his feelings, badly. Even so, he suggested his own alternative plan for another time when they could be alone. But Freda thought he was too controlling, and that was that.

❧

Though Freda came into therapy complaining that men always had to have their own way, she was fortunately able to see quite quickly that Jack had not been making a demand, but an offer — that he was not trying to exclude her mother from her life, but to be given a chance to enter it himself.

With this insight, Freda made swift progress. She began spending more time with friends and enhancing the quality of that time; she encouraged her mother to do the same. Both profited from this shift in emphasis. Pushed out of the nest, Freda's mother got in touch with some remaining grief about her husband's death. Much to her credit, she let go, and Freda was eventually reunited with Jack.

Perhaps the ultimate among controlling mothers is the one who intrudes not only into her daughter's activities but also into her life in such a way as to prevent her from developing an identify.

> Tina's mother had always wanted a daughter to take the place of the sister she never had. After giving birth to two sons and having one miscarriage, she finally had what she wanted, a baby girl. She wanted to make life special for Tina and give her all the wonderful things she had missed in her childhood.
>
> In her earliest years, Tina reveled in her mother's nurturing and constant attention. In grade school she was not quite so pleased by the dresses or with the outings with Mom that sometimes precluded outings with schoolmates. As she progressed in school, she somehow felt she had no life of her own, as her mother became first a teacher's aid in her class and then assistant scout leader for her troop.

In retrospect, what stood out most in Tina's mind as extremely distressing was an event that occurred in the fourth grade, after her mother had begun to do some of her homework. Her mother had particularly liked a vocabulary assignment that called for the construction of sentences using twelve new words. Ignoring the fact that it was Tina's task, and also the age-specific directions, her mother had created a poem that used all twelve words. Then the unwitting teacher had boldly written *A+* and put the poem on the bulletin board for all to admire. Tina kept looking up at this paper with a sense of shame, but most of all she felt lost.

So it went over the years, and although Tina's mother did allow her to do homework as time went on, her domination infiltrated every aspect of Tina's life. Any action Tina took required her mother's approval and consent first; she had no chance to form an opinion — certainly none about the few boys, and later men, she was allowed to date.

When Tina finally started therapy at forty-five, she was still looking for a man her mother could approve of. She was starved for male companionship and for female companionship too — since her mother disallowed most men and included herself in any all-female activities that Tina might manage to arrange. Tina was terrified for her mother to know she was starting therapy.

❀

The early months of Tina's therapy were not unlike exit counseling for cult survivors; her terror at betraying this domineering woman was a major obstacle to her recovery. Even so, after two months her initial decision to keep her therapy a secret from her mother proved to be beyond her ability. Immediately her mother demanded an interview with the therapist, who declined. Then when she asked to participate in her daughter's sessions, Tina felt herself to be in a terrible quandary — which woman to please. It had not occurred to her, of course, to consult her own wishes, so terrified was she of being alone and feeling lost. At last she did, and came up with her own opinion of what was best: independent sessions with her own therapist and conjoint therapy with another. It was a wonderful moment; it was like witnessing a birth — and it led to a new life for Tina.

# 9

# *Unresolved Traumas*

Children, and the adults they grow into, can be traumatized by many things. No matter how loving, no matter how competent, no matter how protective a parent may be, it is impossible to prevent all of the traumas that will have an adverse effect upon a child's life. While many parents like to think that their child is safe, that there is little or no opportunity for trauma, in reality, most children's lives are abundant with potential hazards, some inside the family, and some outside it. Life is hazardous. Many people will have the opportunity to hurt or endanger a child. And some of these traumas will not even come to the parent's attention.

For the adopted child, no matter how much better her life has been made by adoption and no matter how much she is assured of her birth parents' love, there are almost always uncertainties. In ideal circumstances these can be resolved without great pain, but circumstances are often not ideal.

Kay's adoptive family intended to keep no secrets from her. They even kept a scrapbook in which they had gathered important documents and photographs of Kay's biological parents in anticipation of the appropriate time for the disclosure. Many times these loving parents discussed together, and with trusted relatives, how they might present the news, and at what age. But a good time never seemed to come.

In the summer of her tenth year, it was arranged for Kay to spend a few weeks with her favorite aunt and uncle and their children, who were younger than she. Kay liked her cousins, and liked being their babysitter when her auntie had to run errands. On one of those days Kay's little six-year-old cousin was rebelling against Kay's scolding and blurted out the words Kay never will forget: "I don't have to listen to you. You aren't really my cousin. You were adopted."

Kay's aunt was visibly shaken by the disclosure, and not wanting to answer her nieces's urgent question, desperately called Kay's mother. Her mother was stunned and furious at the betrayal, but she was tongue-tied. In answer to Kay's plea for reassurance, she managed to say only, "Yes, honey, it is true." After that she asked to speak to Kay's aunt, and poor Kay heard her screaming with rage all the way across the room.

Driven home the very next day, Kay found her mother no better prepared emotionally to be supportive, and was given little more than cocoa and a scrapbook, tears and an apology. "We wanted to tell you, ourselves" was all her mother could get out. Dad went to get some more tissues, but did not return for several minutes. Finally, it was Kay who opened the scrapbook herself, carefully examining and turning each page, past legal correspondence and court documents, until she came to an unfamiliar photograph.

There was her biological mother, pregnant with Kay. She looked drawn, tired, and tired of being pregnant. Her pose told her story, her hands on her hips seemed like a dare. Cavernous eyes and stringy hair were alien to everything Kay had known as "mother." Mothers had soft bodies, fluffy hair, and pink cheeks. On the opposite page was a photo of her biological father. His arms folded across his chest, he looked for all the world like a movie idol. Again, he was nothing like Kay's image of a father; for the man she knew as Daddy had a chubby face and a potbelly and was safe and steady. Father, mother: What did these words mean now?

In the weeks that followed, Kay's mother told her everything she knew about the biological parents and offered to help her if Kay wanted to locate them. Kay soaked up information about her earliest identity like a sponge and looked forward to the day she would actually meet her birth parents. Kay was absorbing a lot of information and attempting to correct her self-concept, but, almost on overload, she was not expressing many feelings about what she was hearing.

It was not until she was nineteen that Kay took her mother up on her offer and began to search for her biological parents. Unfortunately, the search was not fruitful; Kay's biological mother had died of a questionably accidental overdose of prescription tranquilizers, years before. Her biological father, after a brief incarceration for vehicular manslaughter and drunk driving, had escaped from prison and had never been found. With these discoveries, Kay did get in touch with some of her grief, and even sought counseling for a short time to speed her adjustment.

Ten years later Kay's focus was on turning thirty and having "nothing to show for it." She worked in the escrow department of a bank, "helping other people realize their dreams"; she had few personal contacts in her work, and her social life was dull. She went out on dates occasionally but found her relationships anemic. Sometimes she attended singles functions, trying to breathe new life into a fading flower.

❧

What was truly anemic and in need of attention was Kay's sense of self. She had no firm grasp on her identity. She had no dream other than finding a mate, which she went about in an almost passive way. Through Mr. Right, she believed, she would find fulfillment.

Her traumatic discovery of her adoption had disrupted Kay's ability to form attachments. Reaching inside to find that original pain was both terrifying and exciting; it was also productive. What Kay found was enormous pain about being separated — first, from the woman who had carried her and the man who had sired her, and later from the parents who reared her and betrayed her trust. There was also the loss of her favorite aunt, who never did reconnect with Kay's family. Beyond the pain, Kay found fear and shame. When she looked at the old photographs she wondered: Were they addicts? Antisocial? And most of all she wondered, "Who am I?"

Kay's social life became more active, but not as she had imagined it would in her dreams; it was turbulent, as men became more real for her and she did for them. She began to answer her own questions about her identity. She realized that whatever her genetic inheritance might include, she was neither an addict nor a criminal. She was able to recover the identity of the loving, trusting person who had been thrown off track by a sudden trauma. Seeking a more vital life, Kay made a change of career, and she also found an interesting man.

Another trauma that goes back to the beginning of life is a birth defect. A birth defect can have a ripple effect, stirring up new issues at different stages of life.

Though many children born with defects do not see themselves as defective, a birth defect that is visible or that affects one's speech is likely to create a self-image problem. Understandably the child may be so preoccupied with how she looks or how she sounds that she is unable to develop her own personality — and her difficulties are exacerbated in a culture that focuses on appearances.

For a child born with a cleft lip and palate, Leslie was given the best possible start in life. The delivering physician immediately reassured her eager and anxious parents, explaining that the defect could be corrected and should surely not ruin her life. Early support was also offered by the local cleft-palate team; accurate information about how to feed her and deal with her prospective surgery — and advice about how to survive. Leslie's parents passed that support on to their daughter, staying at her side throughout her recovery from four different surgical procedures. They accepted their baby girl as she was and took photographs of her at every stage. Later they used these pictures to teach Leslie about her early life experience in the hospital.

When Leslie was four years old, her perfect little sister was born, changing the contours of the family forever. Leslie thought she was prepared for this; she had known about it for some time and had looked forward to being the older sister. But now that the baby sister had arrived, she did not feel the way she expected to. She also noticed how relatives and neighbors were making her uncomfortable; they seemed self-conscious — wanting to express their excitement about this new, beautiful baby, but anxious lest they hurt her feelings.

It was during the next year that Leslie started kindergarten and had her first experiences with teasing. Classmates noticed the one scar on her lip and the unusual, nasal quality of her voice. Some just wanted to know about it. Other made fun of her, calling her "harelip" and making bunny faces. Though an attentive teacher brought the teasing to an early end, it made its mark and would never be forgotten. Thereafter Leslie continued to think of herself as defective despite major improvements in her speech. When she was in the first grade, her mother found her many times standing at the bathroom mirror, just staring. "What's wrong, Honey?" her mother would nervously inquire. Leslie had no answer to this question.

It was the question she often asked herself: "What's wrong with me?"

By the time she had reached thirty, Leslie was still asking that question, though the scar on her upper lip was too thin to attract attention and her speech was within the normal range unless she was rushed or upset. She had not been out on a date for several years and had never had an intimate relationship; she had only a few girlfriends she had met at work. None knew her well. Even though very shy in her private life, she functioned well in her career in public relations. Within her prescribed professional role she could bypass her inhibition, look people in the eye, assert herself, and feel relatively comfortable . But within this role, she was promoting her employer, not herself. In a nonprofessional environment, Leslie was lonely and scared.

&#x273B;

Because Leslie had made a decision about herself in the first grade, standing at that mirror, she had to go back to that painful place. Leslie looked again into a mirror, studying her face, gazing into her own pretty hazel eyes. She saw a monster.

During the new few months Leslie came to look more dispassionately at the monster that was so acutely and painfully with her and saw it was not her birth defect, but her anger. She was angry with her parents for having a second child, with the relatives who worked too hard to be polite, with the classmates who spoke in ignorance and fear. And she was furious with God for not preventing all this in the first place. With the emergence of her anger, the real Leslie was back. Angry, but here to stay. She would be working on these feelings for some time to come, but she was not without a relationship for long.

Almost anything that makes a child stand out from his peers as "different" can elicit teasing and is usually managed by the child in the normal course of growing up. Sometimes, however, teasing causes damage because of its severity or relentlessness or the sensitivity of the subject matter.

Franki had always been teased about her name and had no difficulty in rolling with the punches. She had a lot of spunk and a good sense of humor. One boy, however, always got to her. Billy, the class bully. Most of her classmates thought he was funny, especially when he made fun of the teacher; even Franki laughed at some of his antics but he was still the class bully. In the sixth grade, entering puberty, Franki was one of the first girls in her class to develop breasts, and Billy, of course, made jokes about her training bra. It was hard for Franki to set limits on him and to fend off the invasiveness of his humor; and he was beginning to wear her down by February. Her menstrual periods then started one day at school, and Billy, of course, was on hand and the first to notice the red spot on the seat of her uniform. "Look at Franki's skirt!" he called out, and as if this were not humiliating enough, he danced around her, holding his nose and making offensive remarks about her odor. She stood, paralyzed, until her teacher heard the ruckus and intervened.

Billy was reprimanded and sent to the classroom alone to write an apology; Franki's mother was summoned to take her home. In class the next day, Franki was still overwhelmed by a feeling of humiliation and had difficulty concentrating. Her parents noticed that her grades were not so outstanding that year, but they were satisfied that no permanent damage had been done. She had a busy summer and went on to win top honors in the seventh grade.

Photographs from that period tell the tale of the outgoing, spunky girl of earlier years beginning to become careful, rigid, and serious. Franki dropped out of sports in high school, but she was on the debating team and ran for a position in student government — evidence to her parents of a healthy self-esteem. If they had wondered why she had not yet been out on her first date, they did not say so.

At thirty-one, Franki had been out on less than a dozen dates, most of them arranged by friends. She had a relatively successful law practice, built on her growing reputation as a tough adversary. Except for occasional participation in Bar Association activities, Franki's social life was dead. She joked about this in sharing her story, asking "Shall we call the coroner?"

Her humor was alive, and so the coroner was not called. She did seem like a candidate for intensive care, however. After so many years of defensive living, Franki looked considerably older than thirty-one — her shoulders were curling in, she was thin, and she had the habit of sitting with her legs crossed at the knees and again at the ankles. Her jaw was stiff, and her eyebrows almost met in the frown lines over her nose.

Franki's recovery began with reminiscing about Billy's abuse and the damage it caused. Fortunately, it did not require twenty more years for repair. Several months later Franki could drop some of her inhibitions and unload the emotional burden she had carried since the sixth grade. The transformation that followed was astounding and swift. Her feminine side was revived and before long she was romantically involved with someone she met on a cruise ship.

Of the traumas occurring in childhood, one of the most damaging is that caused by childhood molestation. Even when the perpetrator is not a family member, the damaging effects can be horrendous. If the perpetrator is a trusted adult, the effects will be as serious as those of incest.

Justine grew up in a family of decent, hard-working people. She was the last of four children; her closest sibling was a sister ten years older than she. Her parents loved her and often referred to her as their happy surprise. They were baffled when she began to put on weight in the seventh grade, but they said nothing about it. Between the seventh and eighth grades she gained more than fifty pounds and did not stop there.

In her forties, weighing almost 300 pounds, Justine joined Overeaters Anonymous. She found it easy to identify with members who shared their feelings about childhood sexual abuse. She frequently said, "That never happened to me, but I sure identify with the feelings." She considered the possibility that she might have repressed a memory of abuse and often attended public lectures on the subject of molestation, but she was unable to pin down her motivation.

Several years into her recovery, she felt she had reached a block and sought additional help outside OA. She was not seeking help in creating a social life, though she had never been out on a date. She wanted more help with her eating disorder.

Her weight declined steadily as she explored her history with food. But a remarkable shift took place when she was reviewing her twelfth year, the year she was in seventh grade. That's when her appetite flared up with a vengeance. Justine was puzzled because she had remembered the seventh grade as a positive turning point in her life, thanks to her teacher. He had taken a special interest in her and had given her extra credit for staying after school to help him grade papers. She enjoyed reminiscing about her teacher — and blushed and giggled, remembering her crush on this man. One day, without warning, her blush turned ashen, and she sat silent, remembering. For the moment she seemed to stop breathing. Her silence was finally broken with a surprising discovery: "He tried to molest me."

❀

What Justine had repressed for so long was the memory of one momentary lapse by this teacher whom she had so admired and trusted. He had kissed her — not a fatherly peck on the forehead, but a soft, seductive, lingering kiss on the lips. She remembered the shame that registered on his face and how quickly it quieted his erection. She remembered how he begged her not to tell.

Working through her feelings about her teacher's betrayal took a while and brought up a number of unresolved family issues. Her eating disorder, however, became much easier to manage once her silence was broken. The subsequent weight loss brought up additional issues, for as men began paying attention to her, her reactions surprised her. She was angry with these men who "wouldn't give me the time of day before I lost weight," and she was fearful of the great unknown — her own sexuality. In time, however, Justine came to think of these issues as new frontiers, and she continues to move toward them. She is not alone, but in male company.

Divorce is a complex childhood trauma. No matter how well it is handled, divorce represents the death of the family. Moreover, it is so traumatic to the adults involved that they often suffer a temporary regression to an earlier functional level. The loss of the family, coupled with a temporary loss of both parents as a result of their stress, can have devastating consequences for the child.

Gloria was not especially upset to see her parents separate; at thirteen she had seen them part six or seven times, threatening divorce. As usual, Dad was moving out — and as usual to his brother's house, not to an apartment. Gloria was not particularly anxious, for she had observed that when divorce is really impending, one of the parents takes an apartment. Before she went to bed that night, she shed a few tears, missing her father, and wondering whether he would be home tomorrow or on the weekend.

Her first clue that this time things were different came in the morning when her mother went to her hairdresser and came home blond, with a new short hairdo. Somehow

Gloria knew her father had been cut off and swept away, with her mother's hair. Later in the day, when her father called, Gloria tried to cheer him up. She felt sorry for him and worried about how he would take care of himself. There were long silences in their phone conversation; Dad wanted something, and Gloria did not have it to give. Neither of them could hang up. And then finally, a salesman at the door interrupted the call.

Gloria did not feel as sorry for her mother. She was the one who was blocking the reconciliation. But as the days turned into weeks, Gloria's sympathies began to equalize. Seeing her father at the front door, a blubbering mess, whining like a four-year-old, changed the picture; Mom wanted a grown-up, and Dad was a baby. Besides, Mom was sad, so it was hard to think of her as a villain.

Before long attorneys were asking Gloria where she wanted to live. Gloria had her doubts about both parents. Dad seemed too incapacitated to bother with her, and he had also lost his job. Mom seemed to be unloading responsibilities and enjoying her freedom. When it was time to state her wishes to the mediator, Gloria asked to stay where she was, at home with her mother. Mom said, "Good decision," and left it at that. It all seemed unreal.

Five years later, upon graduation from high school, Gloria moved into her own apartment. Although she was being pursued by a nice, reliable boy, she found him boring and moved on to her first dysfunctional boyfriend. Others followed. Two were alcoholic, a few were unemployed, and the rest were depressed. She stayed with each one a while, hoping to make a difference in his life, but ultimately she moved on to the next. She married and divorced three times.

❦

Although many things had contributed to Gloria's attachment to dysfunctional men, her parents' divorce and the subsequent deterioration in her father's functional level topped the list. The guilt she felt in choosing to stay home with her mother, in saying no to her father, was almost paralyzing. She had re-enacted her parents' dilemma over and over again, attaching herself to little boys, trying to fix them as her mother had tried and failed to fix her father. Eventually she became the same sort of angry, rejecting woman her mother had become.

Gloria's recovery required a number of adjustments. She had to correct her misconception of herself as the cause of her father's pain — to realize he was in pain before the custody issue surfaced and that her expression of choice was not the sole basis for the mediator's recommendation. She also had to correct her misconception of her father as the victim — to realize he was an equal partner in the creation of a dysfunctional relationship and that, as his daughter, it was not her role to save him. Although many more lessons continue to enhance the quality of her relationships, these early adjustments initiated the most dramatic changes in her decisions about men. She is now dating someone stable and doesn't seem bored in the least.

Another childhood experience which can have damaging effects is the experience of serial moves. Though living in a variety of environments can be expected to broaden a child's horizons, there are potential negative consequences since the child's secondary attachments outside the family are uprooted over and over again.

> Rosalyn was proud of her father. As a youngster she had carried a picture of him in his Marine dress uniform in her wallet. She missed him when he was sent on a mission, but he always came home. Thank God for that.
> Rosalyn was four when her father decided to make his career in the Marines, and at that age, she had not minded the move from California to South Carolina. There she started school and had no difficultly in making friends; she was even somewhat special as that "California Girl." When her father was transferred to Texas she was in the third grade and the move upset her. They remained in

Texas just long enough for Rosalyn to pick up a significant
accent and a couple of good friends. She was not so
popular in Texas, but she did feel close to her two
girlfriends and had a hard time saying goodbye when
her father was transferred a year later to Virginia.
Rosalyn never liked Virginia, but in the course of four
years she acquired a Virginia accent and also developed
an attachment to a boy at school. Then the family moved
to Southern California, where her father left the service
and entered college. There Rosalyn was popular again.
She fit in well, and her accent made her intriguing. Four
years later, however, when she was in high school, her
father took a position in the San Francisco area, and,
plead though she did to stay with an aunt, Rosalyn was
moved to Oakland.

After graduation Roz returned to Southern California
and began to make a life for herself. She entered a local
community college and proceeded to rebuild her social life.
She enjoyed college as a social environment; she made
many friends among foreign-born students and found a
place for herself in the melting pot. Academically, however,
she did not do well; apparently her low reading skills had
never been recognized or never addressed. After two
difficult semesters she dropped out and entered beauty
school. She excelled both in school and in her first job,
and two years later, with a loyal clientele, she opened a
shop of her own.

By the time she reached her late thirties, Roz had not
married and had no prospects; months would pass
without a date. She was fairly popular among women but
had no close friends.

Roz attended a workshop for chronically single women with a
complex agenda. She wondered whether the paucity of men in her
life might be the result of her limited work environment, and so easily remedied — but she was afraid the cause was much deeper. She

wondered whether her efforts to make friends might be improved, but she could not get over her feelings of being an imposter.

Pet rocks probably have more self-esteem than Roz had at that point. She regarded herself as illiterate and felt much shame on that score. She was self-conscious about her accent and underestimated her natural good looks, which she hid under masses of makeup.

A number of things had contributed to the social drought that brought Roz into a workshop, including the impact of being an only child in a family with no roots, and of having a subservient mother who asked for nothing from her husband but shelter. Clearly the repeated disruption of Roz's social development and the resultant shortcomings of her education had left the biggest scars. In adult life, she coped with her shame by hiding and with her disappointment by controlling her environment too tightly. Making friends and connecting with men will require some unfolding. Roots help people flower.

Children are affected not only by the nature of their attachments to parents and others but also by the nature of their attachments to family pets.

It was MaryAnne's thirtieth birthday that brought home her isolation and prompted her to seek help. Although co-workers had arranged a birthday party for her in the office and her parents and older sister had taken her out to dinner the previous weekend, MaryAnne's birthday had otherwise gone unnoticed. There were no boyfriends to take her out and not even any close girlfriends with whom she could spend the day. She had spent her birthday with her cat, Penelope, whom she considered her best friend. This was her closest personal attachment — the only attachment MaryAnne could tolerate.

There was nothing in MaryAnne's history to explain her inability to form personal attachments — until Penelope, in her own way, provided the answer; she had a stroke and nearly died, an event that opened the door to a crucial part of MaryAnne's childhood, as yet unexplained.

MaryAnne had and lost during her childhood more than a dozen different pets, not counting birds and fish. She could only account for about half of them. One chihuahua was taken to the pound when efforts to housebreak him failed. Another of the same breed was taken to the pound after he bit Uncle Edward's finger when Uncle Edward had insisted on an unwelcome goodbye kiss. One poodle was put to sleep when he developed meningitis; another was taken to the pound because his grooming was a nuisance. Six cats (along with their litters) either disappeared or were taken to the pound. And all these losses had occurred before MaryAnne's adolescence. In her later teens she was asked to dispose of a malamute she had rescued from death at the vet's, because he was damaging her father's rose bushes. Old enough to take some action, she found him a home. When she moved out of the family home she moved to an apartment that did not allow pets. She left her cat, her last pet, with her family and they took it to the pound when MaryAnne failed to find her a home. She felt enormous guilt.

MaryAnne had received grossly dysfunctional messages about attachment and responsibility. And the messages had been made even more grossly dysfunctional by the fact that pets that had been treated with love and tenderness were disposed of at the slightest inconvenience. "I always knew they loved me," said MaryAnne of her family, "but I also wondered if there was a pound for unwanted children who were a nuisance or misbehaved."

❀

In her relationship with Penelope, MaryAnne had practiced what she had always believed, that with love comes responsibility, but there was a long journey ahead before she could trust others to share her belief. Longer still before she could forgive herself for abandoning her last childhood pet.

Her breakthrough came when Penelope finally died and she found that the therapist understood and honored her attachment to her cat, and her grief. Later, group therapy gave her a safe laboratory in which to experiment with relating to others, and it became a bridge, linking her personal island with the larger society.

Whatever the childhood trauma, the magnitude of any residual effects is determined by a number of factors. These include the child's age at the time of the trauma, its severity and duration, the child's mental health before the trauma, the effectiveness of any coping mechanisms employed, and the nature of the family's response. A family responding with support and the willingness to face the trauma head on has a better chance of preventing long-term negative effects. A family in denial or inclined to shame the child for her distress increases the risk of long-term negative effects.

Many things can disrupt a child's growing sense of attachment, or the progression of relationship skills; only a few of the most common have been reviewed. What is important in the life of the chronically single woman is the recognition of the many things that effected personal security, attachment, and identity and expressive skills. It is in recognizing the traumas that disrupted her path to intimacy and exploring her family's response during those difficult times that the chronically single woman can create an opportunity for herself to face these issues as an adult and thus clear and straighten her path.

Even for the woman who has reached adulthood relatively unscathed, perhaps even richly blessed and able to participate in intimate relationships, there are, almost inevitably, traumas yet to come that can disrupt a healthy adjustment and foreclose the use of coping skills that have been developed.

Sometimes traumas are self-inflicted. Extreme feelings of guilt can make a woman think she does not deserve love. Whether her sense of guilt stems from a real or imagined offense, recovery requires an ample measure of self-forgiveness. While some women will find that they have been needlessly assuming guilt for someone else's offense, as is often the case with incest survivors, other women can identify something they did, or something they failed to do, for which they feel a healthy sense of guilt. Seducing a friend's husband, for example, can leave behind serious regrets and remorse. Recovery may require making amends in some way, but it will surely require making amends to oneself for being so punitive.

Most commonly it is abandonment or betrayal that damages women's ability to form and maintain intimate relationships. And betrayal by one man can often foreclose a woman's enthusiasms for intimacy with other men.

> After two years of courtship, a year of engagement, and four years of marriage, Valerie awakened one morning to find Ed gone from their bed. There was a note on the dresser. He could not explain, the note said, but he had to leave and would be back while she was at work to pack his things. In shock Valerie stumbled around their home, readying herself for work — not even questioning, really, whether she could work that morning. She left for work at the usual time.
>
> She had been at work just a short time when, suddenly, her feelings caught up with her. A trusted friend and co-worker found her in tears at her desk. Talking to someone brought Valerie back to her senses. She canceled her appointments and went home hoping to catch Ed when he came.
>
> His closet and drawers were empty. Their emergency cash was gone and so was the portable TV set, even her heirloom jewelry was missing. Ed had not reported for work; nor did he appear at work the next day. Then she discovered their savings account was depleted and bonds gone from their safe deposit box; most disturbing was the discovery that they had been taken several weeks earlier. Ed had been planning his departure for a while.
>
> Valerie's actions over the weeks that followed were not entirely irrational. She had the house locks changed, opened new bank accounts, engaged an attorney and, at

the attorney's suggestion, a private investigator. She also reported Ed's disappearance to the police on the remote chance that he had been the victim of foul play. Privately, she hoped that he was. It was easier to think of her husband as the victim of kidnapping and extortion than to think of him as a willing escapee. Unfortunately, escapee was exactly what Ed was.

The investigator found evidence of large gambling debts, and he also discovered a long-term mistress. Ed had been having a second and separate life, but he no longer had a life at all when the investigator found him. Having sold their car and the other community property he had stolen, he was penniless and homeless and too depressed to make even a slight effort to rehabilitate himself.

Valerie had been in love before, and her closest friends hoped she would love again. Efforts they made to get her dating again were futile. She occasionally agreed to meet a man friends thought she would like, but she never did like any of them, and the men sometimes complained to mutual friends that she had interrogated or otherwise insulted them. Her sense of humor, once a delightful part of her personality, was drifting decidedly toward the cynical and the antimasculine. She was making men pay.

❧

Valerie's anger was understandable; less obvious was the reason she was still in a defensive posture four years later. It became clear, however, that her recovery was slowed largely by her failure to work through her anger. She had been unable even to express it to Ed when she had the opportunity to confront him because he was such a pitiable wreck. She transferred her anger against him to men in general. Even they were not a satisfactory outlet, however, because in addition to being angry with Ed, she was angry with herself: it was not only her confidence in men that was shaken but also her confidence in her own judgement, her confidence in herself. How could she have been with this man, day after day, and not have known that something was wrong? How could she not have known about his mistress? About his gambling? How could she fail to notice that he was no longer attached to her? Restoring self-trust required examining these important questions. It was only after she examined these questions and came to understand her denial that Valerie was able to regain the trust in herself she needed to be open to a new relationship.

Quite understandably a woman whose first love has ended in disaster may lose the ability she once had in relating to men, though most widows, or women "widowed" before marriage, eventually resume the pursuit of male company after a grieving period. Extreme trauma is likely to occur when the death is sudden or the circumstances dreadful. Witnessing a death in a car accident, for example, or by violence will complicate a woman's recovery from the loss, and the cumulative effect of serial losses can be, of course, devastating.

Heidi was no stranger to loss. As a nurse who had lost many patients over the years she was familiar with the impact of death on family members. When her own mother was diagnosed as having an inoperable tumor, Heidi anticipated her own denial, anger, and grief. When her mother chose to die at home, it was Heidi who volunteered to stay with her, helping her mother prepare for death and preparing herself for the loss. She could not fully embrace thoughts of death, however, for soon she and her husband would be holding their first child, the son they had for so long been hoping to adopt. Then, in the summer between her mother's death and her son's arrival, one of Heidi's older sisters had a stroke and died without regaining consciousness. This loss was a severe shock to the whole family; no one was prepared for it.

When her new son arrived, Heidi's attention turned to this new life. She had known no greater happiness than motherhood, and before long she and her husband Rudy began arrangements to adopt a second child, a baby girl in a Third World orphanage. Before the adoption was completed, Rudy was told he had cancer and had perhaps two years or less to live, but after much discussion, he and Heidi decided to proceed with the adoption. It felt important to them to invest in life. Their second child was just under two years of age when Rudy died.

Heidi did not pause long to grieve over these painful losses; she was struggling to adjust to life as a widow and to meet the needs of two little children. Then the unthinkable happened. Her little girl was struck down by a speeding motorist right outside her home, as she stood there helpless and her little boy saw it all — his little sister's head smashed by the blow. Heidi's efforts to revive her were futile.

❀

This poor woman lost four loved ones in less than six years. Although she had expected to lose her mother in time, the deaths of her sister, her husband, and her daughter shattered into splinters her entire adjustment to life. Her childhood training had taught her to trust God — to depend on God for some rational order. "Why?" she kept saying. "This isn't fair."

Fortunately, Heidi's recovery did not hinge on the answer to that question, but on her willingness to ask it. When she took her anger to God, the estrangement ended and a turbulent relationship took its place. When she felt loved and accepted by God, even in her anger, her heart began to soften, and in time she came to feel love and acceptance. Her wish to share life returned.

Yet another woman who may lose her zest for intimacy is the woman who has been sexually assaulted as an adult. It is to be expected that recovery from sexual assault will take time — perhaps a year or more, depending on the circumstances and, of course, the victim's state of mind. When the attacker is someone who is known and trusted, however, the trauma is more complex.

Winnie was not yet over her last failed romance when she went to visit Bill; in fact, she went there seeking emotional support. Winnie and Bill had a long history. Initially lovers, they had parted friends many years before, only to find that they didn't really want to be apart. Their friendship grew, and before long they were best friends. They were both used to hearing about the other's romantic woes; they had seen one another through many a lost love.

Winnie arrived at Bill's house in a sad state, bundled up amorphously in a sweatsuit and badly in need of a handkerchief. She trusted Bill to not care; she had sat with him many times when he was a mess. They were friends.

Bill said the usual reassuring things and stroked her hair as he often did, but his touch was wrong; it was a lover's touch. Upset, she withdrew to the bathroom, and after a few minutes there, thought perhaps she could leave. When she opened the door, there was Bill — who then grabbed her, tore her clothes off, and threw her on the bed.

Later Winnie wondered with regret why she had been unable to say no or stop or anything particularly clear; in truth she had been unable to say anything at all, for she had regressed into a childlike silence and waited, almost without breathing, for him to stop. When he did and she, in silence, got up and dressed and began to cry, he looked at her wide-eyed; he had only then noticed she wasn't with him. On the way home, she pulled to the side of the road, to sob and to vomit; she never saw or heard from Bill again.

❧

After Bill's assault Winnie's choices in men began to change. Previously drawn to seemingly strong, relatively aggressive men, Winnie began to choose boyfriends who were wounded in one way or another — alcoholic, unemployed, or depressed. When they refused to change, she became angry, and then, alone again, miserable.

Faced with so many failures, Winnie did not find it difficult to see that in choosing these nonthreatening men, she was avoiding the feelings associated with Bill's assault. And it was not a long step from there to facing her anger at his betrayal. Working through her anger with him reopened her interest in grown men, and with this, Winnie was satisfied.

What she did not want to explore, but has had to explore, is the reason for her previous attraction to aggressive men and the reason for her regression to a pre-verbal state when confronted by Bill's sexual aggression. Winnie continues today to explore the roots of this spontaneous regression, and when she completes that task, it will be much easier for her to find and love that man in the middle — not the aggressive one and not the weak one, but the one who can be her partner.

Some women lose sight of their relational abilities not because of a sexual assault, but because of a surgical assault. Whether by accident or by design, when a woman's body is altered against her will, even to save her life, she may find it necessary to withdraw from intimate relationships.

> Frances had never been shy — not about sex, or assertiveness, or anything. "What you see is what you get" was always her motto. Her self-confidence attracted healthy girlfriends and boyfriends, and, in her early twenties, it attracted the man she married. They supported each other in building their careers and shared in parenting three children. They had a happy productive life until his death in a boating accident when they were in their thirties.
>
> It took Frances a while to recover from his death; she found single parenthood difficult and worked hard to find that right balance between work and home life. When she found that balance, Frances began dating again. That, too, was an adjustment. "Things between men and women had really changed," she later observed. But she saw finding a

place for herself in a changing social climate was not a difficulty, but an interesting challenge.

Then it happened. Frances discovered a small lump in her breast. She tried not to panic. She phoned a friend who had a benign cyst removed, hoping to hear reassuring words. Instead, the friend encouraged her to take the day off from work and see her doctor. She was still in a daze when her physician sent her off for a mammogram and scheduled a biopsy the next day. Before she knew what had happened, she was signing the consent form for surgical removal of the lump and, possibly, a total mastectomy. She went into the operating room expecting to come out with a modest scar. When she woke up, she felt as though she was in a cast from waist to neck — and she later saw she was bandaged extensively, for her left breast had been removed, along with some tissue from her left armpit.

The months ahead were a nightmare. Radiation and chemotherapy were debilitating and nauseating, and constant reminders of the cancer — and death. Her recovery from the surgery itself was also difficult; the stretching exercises designed to restore the limited function of her left arm were painful. Often she would fold her left arm up into the spaced where her breast had been: it was more comfortable that way. It appeared as if she was curling in on herself, and in effect, she was.

Two years after the mastectomy Frances remained cancer-free and was restored to full functioning. But she did not look the same, and there was a quiet about her. After a while she acceded to the urging of the social worker at the cancer center and began to talk about the experience and her feelings. And she later attended a mastectomy group.

Slowly but surely, a restlessness began to build, and the old Frances began to come back. It was boredom, rather than a readiness for intimacy, that called her back into a social life. But what would she do now? The man

she was dating when the cancer was diagnosed was long
gone. Frances didn't really expect him to stick by her; they
had only begun to date when she found the lump. At a
workshop for chronically single women, she asked, "When
do you tell a potential lover about your mastectomy?" and
then added, "It would make one hell of an ice-breaker!"

Despite her spirit, Frances had a lot to work through
before she returned to the pursuit of romance and remarriage. It was not dating, but going out with girlfriends, that
put her in touch with her pain. And dancing and aerobics
put her back in touch with her body. At last she returned
to her support group, ready to work on a much deeper
level of experience, to be fully honest about her loss. In
her honesty, she found freedom.

❀

The cancer center had offered all the help Frances needed; but
she had not wanted to use it, because it symbolized for her the cancer and the loss, and death. These were the things that Frances had
to face, however, and after a nudge, she found it was the perfect
place for emotional recovery to begin.

Three years later she married.

# Part Three

# SOLUTIONS

# 10

# *Correcting Self-Defeating Behaviors*

Before meaningful change can take place, it is usually necessary to identify the problem and to clarify it — and it is hoped that the preceding chapters have enabled you to identify your problem in a general way. Then you need also to identify your particular pattern as a chronically single woman. Unfortunately this research often requires some repetition of your self-defeating behavior, but it is an opportunity to sharpen your observational skills and to come to know yourself, a *sine qua non* for successful living.

Keeping a journal will be useful — particularly a daily inventory of your relations with men. But its value will be much enhanced if you first make a historical inventory of the men you have dated. Begin with a list of names. Next to each man's name make notes about how he treated you — respectfully or disdainfully, harshly or tenderly; how you felt in his presence — sexy, scared, stiff, happy; how he viewed women — sex objects, ornaments, baby factories, equals; and how it ended. If you have not had any, or many, relationships with men, you can learn much by making a similar inventory of men you have fantasized about. A form facilitating this "Relationship Inventory" can be found in the Appendix.

Now, formally start your journal with an inventory of men who cross your path each day. Again, next to each name make notes, this time about how you responded emotionally at first — attracted or repelled, scared or safe; what you talked about — work, politics, social interests; how you communicated nonverbally — eye contact, posture, touching; and how it ended. You may be able to see patterns in your selection process and your responses already. A form facilitating this "Daily Male Inventory" is also in the Appendix.

Another way of utilizing your journal to create a link with the elusive Mr. Right is to write him letters in your journal. Write down exactly what you are thinking and feeling, no matter how corny or strange, because recovery will come from facing what is, not by putting a pretty hat on it. (Be careful where you store your writing, of course, and with whom you share it.)

As you become increasingly uninhibited in your writing, try setting up conversations in your journal, as a more lively, two-way link with the man in your life. A brief, but revealing, conversation might go like this:

Annalisa: I have no idea what to say to you.
Soulmate: You have always been hard to get to know.
Annalisa: No, you are the one who is hard to get to know.
Soulmate: Tell me what you want to know.

This dialogue brought Annalisa several important insights. It was not he, but she, who was elusive; a power struggle was going on — not unusual in her relationships with men; and when he made himself available, she became fearful. These elements were not explicit in the conversation, but in reading it over, she saw them.

Once you have become comfortable with these techniques for discovering your inner thoughts and feelings, then deal with them directly in your journal. You need not, and should not, try for the best expression of an idea — and you need not, of course, consider what effect the thoughts and feelings you record might have on someone else. Write about them as they come. Go back later — perhaps a few days later, or a month — and read what you have written; look for recurring patterns. For the chronically single woman who does not know how, exactly, she is defeating herself, a journal is an invaluable mirror.

Do not overlook the help available in many communities. Chronically single women workshops can be found in some communities in California, and are specifically designed to identify the nature of a woman's obstacles to intimacy. In addition, workshop sponsors often offer supplementary help in group therapy sessions, led by a therapist, in which chronically single women, by mirroring one another, throw problems into relief and give mutual support. Whether or not a professionally led therapy group is available in your community, you may prefer the leaderless format of the self-help group. You can organize one yourself at little or no cost; guidelines are provided in the Appendix.

When confusion persists, it is time to get individual help from a traditional therapist. Indeed, you will have a running start in therapy, for your journal can be of inestimable value in helping your therapist hone in on your problems. Within a few weeks you should have a much clearer picture of what's going wrong and what can be done to help.

Whatever outside assistance you seek — or even if you seek none — the proverbial recipe for success applies: "How do you get to Carnegie Hall?" — "Practice, practice, practice." And there are tried-and-true exercises that will speed your recovery.

Women whose relationships with men have been thwarted by inhibition and other self-defeating behaviors stemming from fear and shame should practice self-expression. If you are extremely shy with men, start practicing with women. Start wherever you can.

One of the most common symptoms of shyness is the avoidance of eye contact; if you have difficulty on this score, start there. Start with little moments of eye contact, first with women if necessary, and slowly build up your tolerance; if that is too difficult, start by holding your own gaze in a mirror. What do you see? What are you afraid others will see? Notice your feelings, and write about them in your journal. You will find you become daily more comfortable with eye contact, and you will find it rewarding.

It is important, at the same time, to work on dispelling the source of the fear that inhibits your wish to make contact — usually feelings of shame instilled by people who have made you feel unworthy. One person has inevitably started this cycle. Identify that person, if you can, and start there, or start with the first person who comes to mind. Write a letter saying exactly how you have been hurt and why you are angry — not to mail, of course, but for your journal. Allowing yourself a mock confrontation in such a letter gives you some practice in standing up for yourself and an opportunity to unload and clarify some of the feelings that are at the root of your inhibition. It may also help you to decide whether you want a real-life confrontation with the person who has hurt you.

For many women childhood emotional abuse is kept alive in current relationships. For some, the same players are involved: a mother who harps on a weakness or failing — we all have them — or a father who frowns and won't even talk about his disapproval. For others, the childhood abuse is recreated in other current relationships: a boyfriend who, like the mother, is continually displeased about something, or the boss who cannot discuss your weakness in the context of your strengths, or the girlfriend who is sure she knows better than you what you should do and how you should feel. Such perpetuation of feelings of shame must be dealt with, and, again, it's a good idea to start with a letter. You may find, as you review your letter, that the behavior of your boyfriend or your boss or your girlfriend is really not just as it seems, that you are clothing it with experience of the past. But in most cases a confrontation will be necessary.

Deciding how to deal with the shaming boss is a complex matter, but a good place to start, because their reinforcement of shame can be a daily impediment to recovery. It is complex because employers have special rights to criticize and require change, and to fire you if the change is not forthcoming. Abusive language, however, and unfair treatment do not fall within the sphere of the employer's prerogatives.

Dealing with a boss is made more complex by a variety of personal considerations. Do I want to keep this job? Do I need to keep this job? Depending whether you answer these questions yes or no, you will decide to try mightily to work out the problems with your boss, or to chuck the job. In considering the risks involved, you will want to take into account any special protections or assistance that may be offered by the state. And you will want to be sure you are not overreacting because of a childhood history of abuse.

If you decide that a confrontation is appropriate and/or necessary, keeping all these considerations in mind, decide exactly what you want to say, and how you want to say it. Here are a few examples:

> *I am willing to hear your criticisms, but I need to ask you to share them privately, rather than in front of my co-workers (and/or subordinates).*

or

> *Recently, you have brought to my attention a number of criticisms that really concern me. I would like to schedule a time to meet with you and review my performance: specifically, I want to know how you view my overall performance, in light of your recent complaints.*

or

> *I need to stop you right here, because your language is becoming so offensive to me that I doubt if I am going to be able to hear your point. I therefore request that we either table this discussion for another day, give it another try tomorrow, or perhaps invite someone from Personnel to mediate. I am willing to hear your criticisms, but I find your language abusive.*

When your relationship with the people shaming you today is personal, rather than professional, a couple of things are different: they have no inherent right to criticize you; you have no inherent responsibility to listen to them. The nature of confrontations with them will, therefore, be different.

*Stop. I am not available to hear your criticism.*

or

*I am not asking for your opinion about this; I want to form my own.*

When your relationship with someone who is shaming you is close and you want to maintain and foster intimacy, a confrontation will have a very different character. It will be different, especially in that you will be able to temper the confrontation by sharing things about yourself that would be inappropriate to share with others.

*Dad, you say you want to have a better relationship with me, but then you have nothing for me but criticism. All I have ever wanted is your love and respect. Do you have either of those things for me?*

or

*Howard, I've noticed that just when I am starting to feel really close to you, you come at me with some criticism. I find that really distancing; it reminds me of my mother and her negativity, always pointing out my failings. I don't want to wind up estranged from you as I am from her. I want to feel closer to you. Please take a look at what you are doing.*

If your shame stems at least in part from something you have done in the past, then your recovery will require facing it. As you did in writing your letters to people who had made you feel shame, write in your journal exactly what you did and why it makes you ashamed. Again, once you have clarified the issue and gotten in touch with your feelings about it, you can take action. If you have hurt someone, write a letter of apology and mail it unless you feel it would further injure the person in some way. Write a letter to yourself as well, an apology for any shame you have unfairly forced on yourself. A formal confidential confession, encouraged by many religious groups and nonreligious groups as well, can offer further cleansing.

If you are inhibited in responding appropriately in face-to-face contacts, whether innocuous or abusive, it is likely that you avoid them by distancing yourself, thereby missing opportunities. Are you self-demeaning or aloof? Look back, and write what you find in your journal. You will then be able to spot this self-defeating behavior and sometimes find a remedy before a current opportunity is altogether missed. If a man you'd like to get to know was flirting with you at work and you either failed to take notice or responded with some kind of distancing behavior, all is not lost: you can respond the next day.

> *Jeffrey, you were on my mind last night. I think you were flirting with me yesterday, and I'm afraid I might have discouraged you. I don't want to.*

or

> *Jeffrey, was I unfriendly to you yesterday? I didn't mean to be; I was just . . . preoccupied . . . stressed out . . . or what you will.*

You might simply be friendlier, or you might tell Jeffrey you would like to know him better, depending on how distancing you have been before. This may confuse him, however, and some explanation may be required.

If your self-defeating behaviors stem more from an identity problem than from out-and-out fear of contact, then the work you need
to do will be initially more internal. Getting to know yourself,
becoming able to define who you are, is your first task. If you have
been spontaneously writing down your thoughts and feelings in
your journal, you have a wealth of material to start with. Examine
it, as teenagers who keep journals seldom do. But take a cue from
them in another way: experiment. Look through fashion magazines,
and notice your response to different styles. Doing so may help you
define your surface. The newspaper may be a better instrument to
help you explore your interior. What interests you? You will probably find that you know a lot more about yourself than you gave
yourself credit for. Dreams are another wonderful instrument to
help with deeper internal exploration. Start a dream journal, noting every morning even any fragment of a dream you may be able
to recall. If you do not recall many dreams, record your daydreams;
they carry similar significance. If you are in therapy, your therapist
will probably find your dream journal a helpful ally.

As you become more aware of yourself — your thoughts and feelings, your likes and dislikes — you will probably notice you are
more inhibited about expressing some than others. Carry a small
notebook in your purse, and one day each week record some of the
things you think, but don't say. This log will help you see what
parts of yourself you hold back. Do you hold back anger? Or is it
desire? Or is it both? Or is there some subject you're afraid to discuss? If you are in therapy, keep your log on appointment days to
see what it is you withhold from your therapist.

Use your journal to amplify thoughts and feelings you have left
unexpressed. If someone has annoyed you, express your annoyance, or your anger, in a letter — in your journal, not to be mailed.
And if someone has stirred a wish or prompted desire, write a letter about that too. Doing so will release some of your feelings and
temper your fear. As you become more comfortable with parts of
yourself you have been holding back, practice giving them expression. Is it easier for you to express feelings of affection? Or attraction? Or anger? Start by expressing the most comfortable feelings

to the least intimidating person. Be a scientist. Notice reactions, and if you have chosen an unresponsive person, try another. It will become easier to express yourself as you practice.

The woman who practices false advertising has an identity problem, and she is also afraid of expressing herself. Instead of failing to express herself at all, however, she expresses one facet of her personality in the extreme to cover up whatever she is holding back. Recovery involves expressing the whole you. Of course, some judgment is required since there are circumstances in which it is either unsafe, or unwise, to reveal yourself fully. Showing a boss your vulnerabilities, for example, could be self-defeating; showing a mugger your sexuality would be outright dangerous. Recovery involves increasing your access to all of who you are, so that you can make these judgments and express yourself appropriately.

If you are a false advertiser, start with the concept of the human ice cube tray, discussed in Chapter 2. Draw an ice cube tray, and try to name some of the cubes that make up your personality — Brain, Sex Goddess, Trooper, and so forth. Give names of this sort to any part of your personality you can identify. Keep this drawing in a safe place, and add to it whenever you identify another aspect of your personality.

Once you have identified some of your cubes, work on increasing the mutual awareness and cooperation among them. It is important that the different aspects of your personality know one another well and develop the ability to work together. Write down conversations between them in your journal.

> **Brain:** *You embarrass me. I don't like the way you relate to men.*
> **Sex Goddess:** *You are crazy. You don't know how to get men's attention.*
> **Brain:** *But you get only their sexual attention.*
> **Sex Goddess:** *It's better than what you get.*

Early dialogues often lack the spirit of cooperation you are trying to foster; at this point each cube may be fighting for its life. Assure each cube you are not trying to eliminate it but to help it learn to function as a member of the club. As you continue each should learn to be confident of its worth as a member and to respect what the others can bring to the whole. Work toward a blending of these voices.

Another way to work toward integration is through visualization. Imagine what would happen if all your ice cubes were combined in a beautiful crystal bowl and brought to their melting point: the result would be something of a very different nature — easy to serve and pleasant and refreshing for your guest.

Whether or not you feel ready to work on integrating some of your qualities, you can work on using more of them. When you see that you have once again sent one of your cubes out alone to interact with a man, send another after her. Perhaps before The Sex Goddess agrees to one more one-night stand, The Brain can ask to join in.

> *Your offer of sexual attention is not easy to turn down; I do appreciate sexual attention.*

> *It promises a feast, but I end up nowhere with these one-night stands. Do you know what I'm talking about?*

Remember that you are trying to establish a relationship between yourself as a person and someone else as a person also. If the man you are attracted to is little more than a sex machine, your brain will suffer hunger pangs, and you will be discontent. By false advertising, it is just such a one-sided man you will attract. By offering more of yourself, you will attract a man who has more to offer you.

When chronically single women have a tendency to get involved with men who are not available as true partners, recovery requires the willingness to leave these men behind; though it may not be necessary actually to leave such a man, a sound decision must involve a *real* choice, not available to her unless a woman is *willing* to call it quits.

No one can make this difficult decision for you, although many may try. Well-intentioned friends and family members may offer opinions about whether or not this one is worth it, especially those who are tired of hearing about failed relationships. They may, indeed, have valuable insights to offer about what is going on in this particular relationship or about your overall pattern with men, but it is important to pay attention to any hidden agendas they may have. Whether you stay in the relationship or move on, this decision should be made not only for, but also by, yourself.

Many considerations may come into play, so ask yourself a lot of questions — for example: What does this man tell me about his intentions? Does he intend to make himself more available to me? Is his behavior consistent with what he says about his intentions? Is he actively working on making himself more available to me, by way of reading or therapy? Is he actively seeking to make himself available, by way of legal separation or filing for divorce?

For so long as you remain in a relationship with an unavailable man, it would be wise to learn as much as you can from your relationship with him; you don't want to leave him only to find that you create the same dynamic with another man. Ask yourself: Who does this man remind me of? How do I feel in his presence? Where have I felt this way before? Am I indeed making known to him what I want and need? What do I feel when I am with someone more available? Have I readied myself for a man more available for partnership? It is important to listen closely to the answers and to respect them. If you don't like the answers, don't try to change him. He has a right to live his life his own way, just as you have a right to live yours.

During the sorting-out process, when you are trying to find answers to these questions, don't issue an ultimatum of any sort. It can lead only to greater resistance or a commitment under duress, which is of no value. Try changing your behavior. If he is unresponsive in front of the TV, suggest going to a concert in the park; if he is unwilling, go with a friend or by yourself. If he is ignoring you altogether, make some phone calls or read a book. If he is unemployed and not seeking work, don't pay his way; spend more time with friends who can afford to do the things you enjoy. Your needs are your responsibility; so try thinking creatively about how they can be met. Do not wait for him to change: you change. Either he will grow along with you or he will become easier to leave behind.

Though a change in your behavior may work a miracle in your partner and in yourself, it may not. If you have decided to end the relationship but do not feel ready to let go, try writing goodbye letters, just for practice. They will help you to clarify and work through your feelings; they will also help you to anticipate obstacles that might otherwise surprise you and throw you off track — practical obstacles and also emotional roadblocks you or your partner may put up in your way.

If you are currently involved with an unavailable man, you want to create a different future with a man more ready for commitment and intimacy. Prepare yourself for that relationship by writing dialogues with him. Ask that soulmate you desire what is keeping you apart. There is much to be learned from your personal journaling that can create change.

For the woman who remains single because she is preoccupied, recovery requires goodbyes. If someone, or something, stands between you and a partnership, then your choice is clear: let go of what occupies you or stay single.

If you are occupied by a lost love, an unrequited love, or a love for a too-perfect father, again, write goodbye letters. Write as many as it takes for you to realize that the person you have been hanging onto is not there, to face your loss. For some women, these letters will stir up sadness and pain; for others, anger. The grief process that follows — uncomfortable, even painful, though it may be — will help free you from bondage.

The process is more complicated if you are occupied by someone or something that hangs onto you too. When dependency is mutual, as when a parent and a child are enmeshed, saying goodbye to the person may be inappropriate, or undesirable; in this case, it is your *dependency* on the person, or your enmeshment, to which you bid farewell. Typically the person — a father, for example — will react to the change in your behavior negatively. Many people resist change. They find it threatening and may work hard to undermine your progress. If faced with such a response, you will need help. Ask your friends for support; join a supportive group; seek professional help — or all of the above. A therapist is especially qualified to help you explore the roots of the dependency and create a bridge to independent living.

If you are preoccupied by an addictive substance, such as alcohol or some other drug, you will almost surely need outside help to break free: extra muscle. Join a 12-Step program, such as Alcoholics Anonymous, or some other self-help group, such as Rational Recovery, or enroll in a professionally staffed chemical dependency program. Take steps that lead away from addiction and toward intimacy. Also consider traditional therapy, for despite the common belief that a practicing addict is unable to benefit from therapy, that is not always the case; many people have been able to begin recovering from their addictions only after first working on unresolved issues. The door swings both ways. Walk in whichever side is facing you.

Usually it is deeply imbedded relational patterns that cause the door to your heart to revolve, and these are not easy to correct on your own. There are, however, several things you can do to speed or facilitate the process.

If you tend to end relationships abruptly — perhaps prematurely — because you cannot tolerate much intimacy or are afraid of commitment, create some therapeutic space in your life. Spend more time away from the man in your life — with friends or with family or perhaps alone — but away from him. This is a band-aid measure; by itself, it does not heal anything. But it may relieve some of the pressure that has led you to want to bail out. Meanwhile, you can work on your fears.

Whether it is intimacy or conflict or sex you are afraid of, or something else, the roots of your fear are embedded in your history; so start there. Look at photographs of yourself as a child, and look for facial expressions or body language that make you think, "Yes, that's me." Still looking at the picture, write down the feelings of that little girl and identify the people who caused her fears.

> **Mamie:** *I want to understand what is happening to you.*
> **Child:** *What do you mean?*
> **Mamie:** *You get so uneasy when Kurt gets angry.*
> **Child:** *Don't let him be angry with me. Don't let him hit me.*
> **Mamie:** *Honey, Kurt doesn't hit people. Daddy did.*

By reliving the overwhelming fear of her abusive father, Mamie, for example, came to understand that it was that fear and not Kurt's momentary angry look that sent the little girl inside her reeling. She learned to protect and comfort that little girl, who then no longer found it necessary to take flight before she got hurt. Writing dialogues with her inner child gave Mamie a place to begin nurturing herself. Only then did it become easier to get to know and trust Kurt. Kurt was not her father.

It also helps to practice honesty. Rather than putting a guy down because he wants to spend time with you or wants to fight about a problem instead of let it fester, tell him what you are feeling. If fighting scares you, or if a lot of attention makes you feel smothered, or if having sex scares you, talk about your feelings. You don't have to point out what he is doing wrong. He may or may not be doing anything wrong. Figuring out his contribution to the problem is his responsibility. If you can tell him what is happening to you, perhaps you will not have to leave him; that will probably depend on his reaction.

When it is ambivalence that keeps a woman stuck in the single mode, her recovery requires the awareness and resolution of her mixed feelings and uncertainties. Just as in world affairs, internal conflicts are seldom best resolved by a fight to the death. Negotiation is the more effective solution. Look for a resolution that honors all parts of yourself. If you are stymied by a conflict between a desire for intimacy and a fear of abandonment, for example, it is not necessary to destroy your fear: instead look for a way to accommodate your desire in light of your fear, remembering that fear has a rightful place. Perhaps your fear has exceeded its reasonable bounds because your desire for intimacy has been excessive and led you into untenable situations. Start slowly in giving your desire for intimacy expression; consolidate your gains; and proceed. You may find a realm of peaceful co-existence.

Even if you are faced with uncertainty about your sexual identity, the same rule applies: rather than ask yourself how to eliminate your attraction to one sex or the other, ask instead how you may accommodate your wish for commitment in light of your varied sexual yearnings.

The kind of writing that helps best to address ambivalence is dialogue, a dialogue intended to increase mutual understanding and cooperation between the desires that have brought you to a standstill by pulling you in opposite directions.

> **Potential Wife:** *I want to marry Jeff.*
> **Good Daughter:** *Mom and Dad would not like that.*
> **Potential Wife:** *I am tired of waiting for their approval.*
> **Good Daughter:** *Please don't upset them.*
> **Potential Wife:** *What are you afraid of?*
> **Good Daughter:** *I don't want them to leave me.*

This dialogue helped this potential wife to see that the "good daughter" was nothing more than a good little girl — and she was able to form a new concept of what an *adult* good daughter should be. The healthier, adult part was given a voice and it helped her to integrate her fears and become ready to leave home.

None of these exercises, in and of itself, represents a miracle cure for the problem of being chronically single. In using them, however, you can increase your understanding of your problems, while making some significant strides toward a more permanent solution. Allow your own instincts to personalize the exercises to fit your needs. Above all, share your writing with someone you trust. If you are already in therapy, share your writing with your therapist.

# 11

# *Addressing Underlying Issues*

Correcting your self-defeating behaviors will definitely enhance your relationships with men. But a better solution for the long run is to address the issues at work beneath the surface. Ideally, recovery should involve working on both levels at the same time. Correcting your self-defeating behaviors will help you see some of the underlying issues; addressing the underlying issues will make it easier to correct self-defeating behaviors. When women get stuck and fall short of their goals, it is often because their efforts have been focused too much on one level, to the exclusion of the other. Recovery requires dealing with both.

As earlier chapters have shown, those underlying issues can come in many forms. We do not grow up with ideal parents. They are human beings who make errors. Even when parents are close to the ideal they cannot

163

entirely preclude trauma from their children's lives; the amount of monitoring required would cause more problems than it would solve.

As you begin to address underlying problems, your first task is to identify the events that derailed or misdirected your intimacy train. You do not have to identify all the factors at the start, especially if you find the process overwhelming. It would be better to begin by dealing with a few of the more obvious things and allow that work to direct you to the next issue. If you decide to list all your traumas at once, you may find that working on them will lead you to others. Let it unfold.

It is hoped that earlier chapters have led you to identify your underlying problems in a general way. Now you need to focus on your own issues and grasp them fully. Just as your relationships inventory — your review of all of your significant relationships with men — enables you to study your patterns in male/female relationships, so a historical review or significant childhood relationships can enable you to study underlying problems.

To your relationship inventory add lines for your father, your mother, and any other adults who made a significant contribution to your childhood — step-parents, grandparents, foster parents, or others involved in your upbringing. After listing all your significant others, fill in the other columns as before. You can use the "How It Ended" column to indicate where things stand in your relationship with each individual today — turbulent, peaceful, distant, intimate, and so forth; if the person has died, note where things stood at that time.

Expanding your relationship inventory in this way will help you explore the ways in which your choices in men relate to your earliest lessons about men. Are most of your boyfriends like your father, or like your mother? Probably some aspects of each, and quite possibly negative ones — not because we love misery, but because, when we have unresolved issues, we will intuitively be drawn into situations and relationships that enable us to work on those issues.

If you grew up with one abusive parent, for example, and one who passively allowed the abuse to continue, you probably came into adulthood with unresolved issues with each of these parents.

As a result, you may be drawn to abusive men, with whom you will be able to work on your response to abuse. You may also find that some of these men have a passive element in their characters, which will help you get in touch with your reactions to that other parent who sat idly by; meanwhile, you can work on what you are going to do with your own anger.

Another form of writing that helps expose underlying issues is a dream journal. Recording, and paying attention to, your dreams increases your self-awareness. Dreams are the voice of your unconscious. Over time, that voice can give definition and furnishing to your interior. You can expand your understanding of a dream by writing a dialogue with any of the people (or even the objects) in the dream. As described earlier, a dialogue is a conversation between two voices; in this case, one voice is you, and the other voice is the person or object you wish to analyze or reckon with. One patient had a dream in which she was being chased by a huge, red tomato:

> **Lena:** *Who are you?*
> **Tomato:** *Don't be so demanding.*
> **Lena:** *I am only asking your identity.*
> **Tomato:** *It was the way you asked.*

Before too many more lines, Lena recognized the voice of the tomato as her controlling mother. Later, it was revealed to be her own femininity: red, ripe, and on a roll. It terrified Lena. She associated her own womanhood with her whiny, victimy, yet domineering mother. She was eventually able to befriend the juicy tomato, and make it hers. Her healing was facilitated by additional dialogues with the tomato, along with letters to her mother, focused on differentiating herself.

An autobiography will further help identify underlying issues. Traumatic experiences that you have not yet identified will emerge — but it is important also to look for themes. Are you writing mainly about hard lessons? Or disappointments? Or losses? Or betrayals? Or compromises? Or white knights?

If you should happen to come up relatively empty-handed,

extend your inventory to some of your significant relationships in adulthood — especially noting anyone who may have hurt you. Expand your autobiography to include some of the traumas of your adult life. You may find your answers in more recent years.

For some women the process of exploring old wounds is terribly confusing. They may wonder, "Was there really anything wrong with my life? Or am I just crazy?" For some it can be even more painful than the original trauma. There is a reason for this: Children find some way to adjust to their circumstances; many, even in the worst of circumstances, see nothing wrong with their families. They see only what they need to see to survive. The full impact of the trauma may only become apparent now.

The purpose of identifying life experiences that have derailed your intimacy train is, of course, to get over them — to deal with them in such a way that they will no longer have a negative impact on your life. To accomplish this purpose, many women turn to professional help. If it feels important to you to proceed without help, ask yourself why. What did you learn in your childhood about getting help? Was it shameful? Or perhaps pointless? Perhaps shunning help is itself a dysfunctional pattern.

Remember that your recovery involves not only an improved relationship with yourself but also an increased ability to relate to others. Start breaking your self-defeating patterns as soon as you can. If trying to do everything all by yourself is one, start there.

As you begin to identify some of the life experiences that have made intimacy difficult, the time has come also to deal with the impact of those experiences. And just as writing letters can be helpful in clarifying and dealing with feelings, so also they can be helpful in understanding traumas.

If it is loss you must deal with — death, abandonment, and divorce, as well as the loss of health, beauty, or even some part of your body — start with a goodbye letter.

> *My Dear Left Breast,*
> *I can still hardly believe that you are gone. Sometimes,*
> *especially when I awake in the middle of the night, I swear I*

*can feel you. I even begin to roll over, fully expecting to feel*
*you pressing into my chest, and, in fact, feeling you there.*
*But I continue to roll. And the feeling fades. You are gone.*

*Yesterday, a guy I work with was staring at the space you*
*once occupied. He is a nice guy; he didn't mean to be rude.*
*But I hate the way everyone knows you are gone. I hate their*
*being curious. I hate the way they treat me — differently —*
*like an invalid. Isn't that the perfect word? Invalid. Am I still*
*a valid woman?*

A woman who lost a breast wrote many letters before she found
answers she could live with. Her first letters, which she began to
write six months after her mastectomy, allowed her to overcome her
denial of her loss. Six months later she was finally able to say her
farewell. In between there were letters to the surgeon, to the
boyfriend who had left while she was in the hospital, and a few letters to God. She had a lot to say.

In some cases a loss is complicated by other issues that are
associated with it. A woman whose face was disfigured in a childhood accident suffered not only the loss of her beauty but also the
indignity of teasing in childhood and the excruciating pain of being
shunned by peers in adolescence and adulthood. While surgical
repairs restored most of her physical beauty, only emotional repair
could make it safe for her to attract attention. She had angry letters to write.

Losses can also come in the form of disappointments, anything
from a series of household moves to the relapse of a recovering alcoholic parent. In serial moves, it is the attachment to friends that is
lost; in the case of the parent's relapse, it may be the parent who is
lost. Disappointments come with pain, and the pain must be worked
through. Again, letters can help. Sometimes it helps to write the letter from the perspective of the child who was disappointed.

*Dear Daddy,*
*When I came home from school today, you were gone. He*
*was back. He had been drinking all day, I think. He smelled*
*bad, and He had wild eyes. I went to find Mom, but she*

*wouldn't look at me. She was washing clothes, and her eyes looked all puffy and red, and she asked about my day at school, as if this was just another day. As if nothing's wrong. Something is wrong.*

*Daddy, where are you? Where do you go when He is drinking. I need you. He scares me. He hurts Mom, and I know He will hurt me, too. Why can't you help me? Why do you let Him take over?*

Letters like these helped this wounded woman come to terms with the disappointment no one would speak of, which she came to understand as the loss of her father to alcoholism. Early letters were marked by alternating pleas for help and cries of anger; later letters of anger were directed more at the disease of alcoholism, which was killing her father. Then she recognized the loss of her mother, as well, to depression and to the disease of co-dependency.

Losses also occur in the form of betrayals — abandonment, sexual abuse, infidelity, or any action that breaches a covenant. Betrayals are complicated, for they involve not only the loss of the individual who betrayed you but also the loss of trust in covenants. They cause deep wounds; again, however, confronting your emotions can help bring about healing.

*Mother:*

*Oh, how I have always loved the sound of that word. I imagine loving it from the very beginning. I imagine floating in your womb, safe, warm, loved, wanted. I imagine your hand resting tenderly on your stomach, feeling me kick and wiggle, or sometimes feeling me sleep. We were as one. I lived in you.*

*But my time came to be in the world, and everything changed. I wonder how early I knew; I wonder when I realized that you would not keep me. I wonder when I realized that the woman who fed me and rocked me and changed me was not you.*

*I hate life out here. Out here it is hard, and drafty, and dif-*

*ficult; in you it was safe and warm and wonderful. I want
back in. Let me back in.*

Earlier letters to the woman who gave her up for adoption were
marked by anger and questioning. This letter was written during a
period of longing. They weren't just about adoption. They were
about being kicked out of the garden. Through them this woman
was able to let go and to live in the world.

Because the pain associated with the loss of a person or a part
of one's physical self is acute, the loss, though difficult to deal with,
is in most cases readily identified. A gradual loss of one's emotional self is often hard to recognize, however. Usually it stems from
childhood violations of personal boundaries that a dependent child
has no choice but to tolerate — and the tolerance can build up and
become habitual. Recovery will therefore require some work on
your personal boundaries.

A boundary is that invisible, protective barrier around you that
defines for outsiders just how close they are allowed to come. In a
healthy person, a boundary is firmly placed but flexible; it can be
strengthened to defend you against unwanted attention, and it can
be softened to admit desired attention. Unfortunately, boundaries
can be crossed without your consent. When this happens, women
may react by severely restricting access to themselves, or by abandoning their boundaries, letting even flies in. While working on the
establishment of healthier boundaries, it is important to work on
the violations causing the problem.

If you find yourself becoming enraged by behavior that feels like
an invasion of your boundaries, take note. Are you overreacting and
on the verge of taking some self-defeating action? Are you swallow-
ing your rage and playing the role of victim — an equally self-
defeating response?

To deal with adult violations of privacy as an adult, you must
also be prepared to deal with the unresolved childhood violations
from which your reaction stems, the helpless rage of your inner-
child. But the experience is diffuse and hard to grasp.

Start by writing a letter in your journal to the person who has precipitated your rage, as Mary did to her boss, pouring into it all the rage she then recognized as directed toward her mother.

> To: The Boss From Hell
> From: Mary L.
> RE: Butting In
> Having tried every tactful way I can think of to tell you to butt out, I now resort to being blunt: BUTT OUT!!!! I do not know why you have to interrupt every frigging conversation I have, but it is going to stop right here. You are on notice that I am a separate person and that you are not welcome in my every encounter — only by invitation. There is no standing invitation. Get it? From this day forward, if you butt into a private conversation, I will tell you RIGHT IN FRONT OF THE OTHER PERSON that this conversation is PRIVATE. If you want to talk to me, make an appointment.

Subsequent letters to her mother emptied Mary of rage, enabling her to effect appropriate confrontations with both mother and boss.

Even closer to home is the anger aroused by the person who damaged your identity in childhood and continues to do so — either by an outright takeover, such as controlling your career, or by a dependency that invades your personal life. This, Sandy's dependent mother did by telephoning at eight on Saturday mornings and asking, "Did I wake you? Are you alone?"

Determined to put a stop to the invasions, Sandy made an effort to grasp the problem by writing a practice letter to her mother in her journal. In the two-and-a-half pages it took to write the letter, Sandy was able to see for herself that she still felt like a child. It was a letter from a child to her mommy, full of explanations and fear of abandonment.

This letter stirred up a lot of Sandy's pain. But as these feelings passed, she was able to re-write her request. After two more tries, the letter was reduced to one line:

*Mom, don't call me before 10:00 A.M. on the weekend.*

Sandy decided to add:

> *. . . and do not ask me if I am alone; that is not something I care to discuss.*

If one's identity has been almost annihilated, as Sandy's had by her mother, there is much work to be done before boundaries can be established — first grieving for all that was lost in childhood and then defining one's identity. There are many ways of getting to know yourself, some of which are mentioned in the last chapter. Study the thoughts and feelings you have written about in your journal. Experiment with new styles of dress. Notice what newspaper articles catch your interest. Watch your dreams, and listen to your heart. And don't forget to notice qualities you admire in others.

Then it is time to start establishing boundaries.

Sandy's actual confrontation with her mother seemed to go well. Her mother had one or two questions about the new boundaries, which Sandy was able to field with relative ease. A few days later, however, a three-page letter came in the mail from her mother, pouring out copious amounts of rage and defensiveness.

Before responding to the letter, Sandy took time to look back over her history with her mother, in reverse chronological order, starting with this recent letter. Ultimately she found her way to her resentments about her childhood and released her anger. Sandy was then able to meet with her mother and state her case. It was important to her to not replicate her mother's behavior. She wanted to be different. She wanted to be her best self. And her final letter to her mother freed her to be just that. It was a letter to her mother's inner child:

> *Dear Baby Helen,*
> *As I sit down to write to you, I picture you as a thin, frail baby with dirt on your face and no one to love you. A woman has left you in a tattered basket on my doorstep. I want to run. I fear the responsibility laid on my doorstep. I don't want it. But can I say to you "I don't want you?"*

*That is not what I want to say. What I want to say, and
have to say, is that you are not mine. I do love you, I pity you.
I know what it is like to not have a good Mommy. You and I
both deserved very much to have good Mommies. But neither
of us did. Knowing that you could never mother me, I have
found other Mommies for myself. I have found one in my therapist and others in my mentors; I have found one in an old
friend. One day I found one in myself. I know now that I am
going to be okay.*

*But I am not going to be your Mommy, little one. I will
always love you and hope that you, too, find Mommies to
help you love yourself. I give you back to the woman who left
you on my doorstep.*

*With love and best wishes,*
*Sandy*

With this writing came a lot of pain — the pain of compassion,
as well as the pain of Sandy's deprivation. With tears, she let her
mother go. There would still be the odd skirmish from time to time,
but Sandy had back her spirit. In recovery she was able to establish healthier boundaries, not only with her mother but also with
others. Her new boundaries were firmly in place but flexible; she
was able to strengthen them as needed to defend against unwanted attention or intrusion and to soften them when it was her desire
to let someone in.

Long-term recovery from being chronically single generally
requires dealing with family and traumas that cause your self-
defeating behavior. When those issues involve parental inadequacy
or abuse, then, like Sandy, the woman must not only address her
memories and feelings but also develop her own internal parent to
help compensate for the loss. Developing an internal parent is
nothing new; it is what adulthood has always been about: using the
best of what you have internalized from the past. Once the issues
and traumas have been addressed, the chronically single woman
must look to decisions she made before she resolved things, for
these decisions may still be adversely affecting her life.

# 12

# *Sharing Life*

Sarah entered therapy at the age of thirty-five with the encouragement of old friends who were concerned about her emotional state. She was moody and irritable and seemed to be chronically in a state of crisis about money, about her job, or about her relationships. She was sleeping poorly and waking in the early morning not feeling rested. In addition, her energy level seemed to be dropping steadily. She complained of a decline in her social life, which she related to her poor self-esteem. She didn't feel worthy of company, she said. Sarah looked tired; she was pale and had dark circles under her eyes. She wore a navy blue business suit, slightly enlivened by a turquoise lapel pin. She appeared to be making an attempt to look better than she felt.

Eight years after a divorce from a man who had abused her, body and soul, Sarah was very much alone.

She had no steady relationship with any man, nor had she for three years, and she was alienating even her best friends through her moodiness. Sarah wrote: "I am unhappy with myself . . . afraid to be myself around males — if I can figure out who myself is."

Sarah had sought help in therapy before, during her turbulent marriage. She remembered her therapist as a sort of guardian angel — someone who helped her define her husband's sexual abuse as marital rape and encouraged her to leave him. Sarah left her husband, and moved out of the area with great hopes for the future, but she was leaving behind her therapist as well as her husband.

A year later, when she was having difficulty establishing relationships with men, Sarah again entered therapy, hoping to break away from her dysfunctional patterns. Her new therapist was an older man, in whom Sarah had confidence. When his responses seemed sometimes mildly flirtatious, she thought she must be imagining things. As time went on, she thought she was perhaps special to him in some way. She felt she was making progress in understanding her dysfunctional efforts to be a good wife, for example, by accommodating her husband's perverse sexual impulses. One day the therapist remarked, "You were the little vixen, weren't you . . ." Sarah did not know what to say. She continued to see him for several weeks, not knowing how to respond to his offers of physical comfort until she ran from him in shame after he actually seduced her.

Sarah blamed herself. She felt great remorse at the thought that his wife might have been wounded by their one-night stand. She assumed all responsibility, denying any anger or pain. In fact she idealized the therapist; she regretted that her discomfort made it impossible for her to continue seeing him. Even when given a formal printed document outlining the legal code prohibiting therapists from engaging in sexual activities with their patients, she was unable to accept the notion that her rights had been violated.

As Sarah's therapy continued, it became apparent that she was, in a way, more uncomfortable in being confronted with this notion by a female therapist than she had been in being victimized. She had no prior experience simply asserting that a man's behavior was unacceptable. Women had "explained" men to her, or excused men to her, but had never shown her how to assert the simple truth with men.

Sarah was the older of two children born to a remarkably unhappy couple. Her father was a verbally abusive alcoholic who continued to be abusive to Sarah in her adult life. Nothing she did pleased him, and he expressed his disapproval in the most vulgar and hurtful of ways. Her mother, whose ability to cope with her husband's antics had always been a mystery to Sarah, had an affair when Sarah was in her teens and subsequently left her husband, taking Sarah with her. One year later she died in a car accident, and fifteen-year-old Sarah went to live with her father and step-mother.

It was then that Sarah's father confided in her that, like her mother, he had had an extramarital affair while Sarah's mother was pregnant with her. Whether he was totally indifferent to his daughter's feelings or intentionally sadistic didn't matter. His revelation had a very adverse effect on Sarah. By association, Sarah remembered an earlier trauma — being molested at the age of five by a family friend — and she was told by her father to forget it. When she appealed to her mother, she was told not to upset her father by discussing the incident. She complied. Sarah always complied. She was a very good girl.

Neither parent demonstrated concern for their little girl; their responses were focused exclusively on their own needs. In this instance they taught Sarah several painful, life-altering lessons: that her needs were not a consideration; that talking about her pain and distress was pointless; that, for the welfare of her parents, it must be forgotten; and, perhaps worst of all, that a male could sexually abuse a female at will, with impunity.

Sarah was able to find an escape from this dysfunctional family only in an early marriage. She wanted a different kind of life.

As years went by, however, the marriage deteriorated as her husband's drinking and sexual demands increased. When drinking, he became a veritable Mr. Hyde — belligerently picking fights and sadistically flaunting his extramarital sexual forays in front of Sarah. Then came increasingly sadistic sexual behavior, often including oral and vaginal marital rape — and there was even an attempted gang rape, which her husband tried to organize with a few of his drinking buddies. Sarah's attempt to discuss these events came with an overwhelming sense of shame because she blamed herself for all the hardship that had befallen her. She also experienced considerable tension and nausea. It was a time of purging.

Weeks passed, and Sarah began to reflect on the other men in her life. Her inventory of her many failed attempts to establish relationships with men after her divorce revealed a pattern of attraction to men who were afraid of commitment — several of them alcoholic and needy. She had repeatedly played the role of caretaker, giving them the attention she was ashamed to admit she needed.

Sarah began dating again, and who should start courting her but a man who seemed the opposite of all the others. He showered her with attention and gifts and with constant avowals of interest. This was a new experience for her, and reassuring, although she did not find this man particularly attractive. Sarah wondered whether she should stay with him and give him the benefit of the doubt; he seemed to be the stable, financially secure, emotionally available man she had been searching for. She felt that somehow she was at fault for not finding him attractive and accused herself of sabotaging her own recovery. Being urged to look closely and to listen to her instincts, she was able to see within just a few weeks that he also was a terribly needy man. He was showering her with attention merely to gain his own ends and was wholly intent on the fulfillment of his own needs, not hers. He would give Sarah whatever it took to get her to take care of him. Rejecting him did not come easily to Sarah, but it was easier than had been the rejection of her husband. His name was the last on her list of self-absorbed users.

It was during work on these relationships that Sarah had her biggest breakthrough. Having seen it in stark outline in her last suiter, Sarah developed the perspective she needed to see the neediness of her other partners — their sense of entitlement and their inability to relate to her needs. She then expanded her inventory beyond boyfriends. She listed "the family friend" who needed gratification and power and felt entitled to fondle an innocent little girl. She listed her father, who needed to hurt and control others and felt entitled to expose Sarah to his every thought and feeling without regard for the cost to her. Finally, she listed her former therapist, who needed gratification and power and felt entitled to take what he wanted from Sarah.

Looking at her list, Sarah was furious. She wanted to make those men pay. "Pay for what, Sarah?" she was asked. "Pay for hurting me," she answered, and with this acknowledgment, pain finally came into her voice. Soon afterward, the tears came, and then she grieved for all that she had lost at the hands of the men in her life. With her tears she shed the unwarranted shame she had carried for so long and found the voice her parents had silenced when she was five. She decided to hold others accountable for their behavior. She reported her former therapist to the licensing bureau and filed suit against him for damages. She was successful on both scores — but perhaps her greatest success was her confrontation of him, in which she was supported by her attorney.

A significant shift had occurred in Sarah's perception of herself. She no longer saw herself as a victim. It was as if chains were being cast off. She lessened her involvement with her family, and the real woman began to emerge. She began to come to life. Her anger had put some color on her cheeks. The cash award she received for damages enabled her to expand her wardrobe, and her new clothes expressed a colorful, soft, and sensual woman. It was safe to be female. She attracted a lot of positive male attention. Before long, she attracted the attention of a man named Matt.

Sarah and Matt met at a party. There was immediately a positive chemistry between them. They danced and made plans for a date the next weekend. Having invited him to escort her to a large party, she waited for him to call for her with a mixture of happy anticipation and apprehension: she found him very attractive, and she was afraid he might disappoint her.

Matt arrived on time, wearing a tux, and carrying a flower. He looked gorgeous in his tux, and he was poised and charming throughout the evening. "He is perfect" she thought — and this terrified her. The next morning she awoke in his arms, more satisfied than she had ever been before, and happy — and panic went through her.

She had given more of herself than ever before. Was this a mistake she might regret the rest of her life? Surely pain would follow. Surely he would abuse her in some way. Would he abuse her with some humiliating review of the night just past? Would he pick this moment to inform her that he had AIDS or herpes? Would he abandon her?

He poured some orange juice and made toast and coffee. Though he surely felt her tension, he did not comment on it or inquire about it. To Sarah, the whole thing seemed unreal. He continued to ask her for dates, and she continued to be tense. "Something is wrong with this guy," she kept thinking — and she found fault. She complained about his being late to pick her up and about his falling asleep while watching a movie; she complained about innumerable things.

Though patient, Matt eventually confronted Sarah. He wanted to know what was going on with her. He wanted to help her, and he also wanted her to treat him with more consideration. This blew her away. He was not about to abandon her. He wanted to understand what was troubling her, and he wanted her to know he had some special sensitivities. He had been molested as a child by a babysitter, he told her, and although he had received therapy, it was still difficult for him to respond to anger or aggression in women. For a moment, Sarah was speechless. She could have said, "Me, too," but for Sarah that was too difficult. Finally, she broke the silence with words of support for him.

In the months that followed, much of Sarah's therapy focused on her struggle to let Matt in. For many weeks she talked about occurrences that seemed to point to failings or faults, justifications for leaving him. Then she would giggle nervously, blush, and say "Oh, he's not so bad, is he . . .?" She was beginning to recognize her fears of intimacy, but she was at the same time struggling to learn to share life with a man.

It was not only fear of intimacy that began to rock their bed, however. Despite their blissful introduction to shared sexuality, Matt and Sarah ran into increasingly severe barriers in the bedroom. No matter how tenderly, how carefully, Matt approached her, at some point in their love-making Sarah would shut down. Sometimes there was a barrier to arousal for Sarah, and sometimes, having been aroused, she was suddenly filled with rage. When Matt tried to talk with her about what was happening to her, she lay silent.

Recognizing the signs from his own experience, Matt asked, "Was it your father, Sarah?" His question blew her away. She said "No, it was my ex-husband." With this, she began to cry; for the moment, the hostile impulses vanished. Sarah was not yet ready to talk about being molested, but she was talking with Matt about her struggle. And she was letting him support her.

These difficult times in the bedroom motivated Sarah to work on her unresolved feelings about being molested and about her parents' painfully disappointing response to the crisis. Focusing on what it had meant to be a victim and to continually view herself as a victim freed Sarah to be more than a victim. More chains were cast off.

The time had come for Matt to meet Sarah's family, her father, step-mother, and step-siblings. She was prepared, and she prepared Matt for the drinking and abuse he would witness — but she was still filled with apprehension. Would Matt embarrass her? Would her father? Would Matt be able to take care of himself? Would she?

Matt made her proud, and her father could not embarrass her because Matt interrupted him before he could finish any abusive remark, and Sarah followed suit. Faced with this powerful couple, her father backed down. Sarah had learned to take care of herself, and as she showed more and more self-respect, others respected her, too. Her father even began to apologize from time to time. Her step-brother and step-sister, who had never acknowledged Sarah as a sibling, began to welcome her in their homes as a sister. She had acquired a family. Not a perfect family, by any means, but a family.

Grief followed, however, for Sarah realized her father would continue to drink and be thoughtless and downright mean; her step-mother would continue to be aloof at best, and often mean. They would never change. Her efforts to set boundaries would only be successful in the moment; she would have to reinforce them with each visit. There would never be a mother to show her how to deal with all this — a fact she thought she had accepted long ago, but she had not, and so was very sad.

Sarah explored her reactions to her father's alcoholism and verbal abuse in many letters, and she found anger in them and sadness at her loss. She would never have the father she wanted, and finally she came to accept that as fact. Then she began writing letters to her deceased mother, exploring the mystery of who this woman was. How did she cope? Why didn't she step in to help her children, to protect them from their father? Sarah then wrote a dialogue, giving her mother a voice, inviting her mother to answer the questions that had plagued her for so long. In doing so, Sarah found in herself the voice of a nurturing parent — not the voice of her mother, of course, but her own. She was finding and cultivating her own maternal instincts and learning that she could nurture herself.

Sarah's insecurities did not evaporate. She arrived one day at her therapy session wearing an engagement ring — and she felt still so fearful that her happiness would somehow be taken away that she did not mention it. She had come far enough, however, to trust Matt and herself.

The barriers that had closed her off in the bedroom came down, and with that Matt realized he still had some sexual barriers of his own and returned to therapy. They were helping and nurturing each other.

Now they are married. They are not happy every day, but they are together every day. They are partners.

# 13

# *Journey Out Of The Singles Trap*

Your journey may be unlike any of the women In this book. I have not met two women yet who had the same story or the same requirements in recovery. Each of us is unique. While this book, and others, may give you ideas about issues you need to examine and suggest exercises that may seem promising, there is nothing so immediately helpful, or as sensible, as looking at the obstacle in front of you and starting there. I encourage you to do just that.

***Honor your past and present relationships.*** We all have to face the past. As others have observed before, those who refuse to face the past are destined to repeat it. Facing the past, however, does not mean punishing yourself for the dysfunctional relationships you may have had along the way, or may even be involved in now. Punishing yourself is of no use whatsoever; it will, in fact, slow your progress. Know that you have, or have had, these relationships for a reason. Learn the lesson each relationship has to teach you, and move on. Punishing others will not help you, either. Having and expressing your anger doesn't mean blaming others or harboring resentments against them. It means facing obstacles and putting them behind you.

*Build on your willingness to be known.* You do not have to wait until you are free of all pathology to make friends and loved ones and settle down. Find friends with whom you can share your journey — and share it. Let "safe" friends know what you are experiencing as you work on issues you are trying to resolve. Let yourself learn from their experience; let them learn from yours. It's not just that you don't have to go through this recovery alone; you can't. Start with something as simple as sharing with a girlfriend your weariness at being alone. You may then feel like sharing your reactions to the information in this book, or perhaps some of the writing exercises. Before long, you will be and have an intimate friend.

*Deepen your existing relationships.* You probably already have people in your life who can identify with the issues you are thinking about. Some may be only superficial acquaintances, and others may be good friends. It is amazing, though, what good friends can avoid talking about. Choose one friend and practice letting her closer. Then another. You will also be getting closer to her, establishing a real relationship. You will be able to ask for support and encouragement when you grow weary of the journey, and you will be able to give it. We all need friends we can answer honestly when they ask, "How are you?"

*Deepen your relationship with yourself.* Your relationship with yourself lasts your whole life through. Others come and go, but as long as you live, you have you. Do not be fearful of knowing yourself; be accepting of your mistakes as you would those of a friend. And just as you enjoy a friend more as you know him or her more deeply, so you will come to thrive on self-knowledge. And so you will develop self-love. Remember that, in general, others will treat you as valuable when you come to value yourself.

***Live in accord with your heart.*** Remember the oft-quoted Shakespearean precept, "to thine own self be true." And remember that it is *your* life you are living. If you feel called upon to share it with a mate, do so. If you feel called to share your life with a particular man, then even if others disapprove, do so. No one can know you as you can know yourself. No therapist can select the right mate for you, no friend or family member. Love whom you will.

***Let your real, whole self attract whomever it does.*** Chronically single women too often defeat themselves by giving what they think men want instead of giving them who they are. This is the road to misery, not the road to a happy marriage. The man you attract when you are your whole self will be a much better partner in life. His relatedness will not stem from some shallow image that will disappear, but from a three-dimensional you.

# APPENDICES

# Appendix A
## Relationship Inventory

| Men's Names | How They Treated Me | How I Felt In Their Presence | How They Viewed Women | How It Ended |
|---|---|---|---|---|
| | | | | |

# Appendix B
## The Daily Male Inventory

| Name | My Internal Response | Verbal Interaction | Non-Verbal Interaction | Result |
|---|---|---|---|---|
| | | | | |

# Appendix C

## Starting A Self-Help Group For
## Chronically Single Women

1. Select an optimum meeting day and time. Remember that most participants will be employed, requiring an evening or weekend meeting.
2. Identify a meeting place. Free or low-cost meeting rooms can be found at churches, libraries and hospitals. Some communities have a women's center, which may be able to offer not only space but also eager participants.
3. Identify referral sources. Consider placing a flyer in places frequented by women. Hair salons and gynecologist's offices are both good choices; these are places women tend to be candid, and therefore receptive to new ideas. Check your local newspapers for options; in addition to placing a classified ad, you may have access to a column in the community affairs section listing local support groups and clubs.
4. Prepare a meeting format. Identify one or two options to present to your groupmates at their first meeting. Allow the group to choose. Your group may elect a 12-step format; in this case, obtain consent and guidelines from Alcoholics Anonymous. If the group prefers to form an independent self-help group, you can obtain a sample flyer and meeting format from the author. Send a self-addressed, stamped envelope to:

Karen Jenkins, MSW
P.O. Box 5946
Orange, CA 92613-5946

# Suggested Reading

Bass, Ellen, and Laura Davis. *The Courage To Heal: A Guide for Women Survivors of Child Sexual Abuse.* New York: Harper & Row, 1988.

Beattie, Melody. *Codependent No More.* Center City, MN: Hazelden Foundation, 1987.

Bradshaw, John. *Bradshaw On: The Family.* Deerfield Beach, FL: Health Communications, 1988.

Carlson, Kathie. *In Her Image: The Unhealed Daughter's Search for Her Mother.* Boston: Shambhala, 1990.

Cermak, Timmen L. *Diagnosing and Treating Co-Dependence.* Minneapolis: Johnston Institute Books, 1986.

Cohler, Bertram J., and Henry Grunebaum. *Mothers, Grandmothers, and Daughters.* New York: John Wiley & Sons, 1981.

Covington, Stephanie, and Liana Beckett. *Leaving the Enchanted Forest.* San Francisco: Harper & Row, 1988.

Cowan, Connell, and Melvyn Kinder. *Smart Women/Foolish Choices.* New York: Crown Publishers, 1985.

Drew, Jane Myers. *Where Were You When I Needed You, Dad?* Newport Beach, CA: Tiger Lily Publishers, 1992.

Erikson, Erik H. *Identity and the Life Cycle.* New York: W.W. Norton, 1980.

Fischer, Lucy Rose. *Linked Lives: Adult Daughters and Their Mothers.* New York: Harper & Row, 1986.

Fossum, Merle A. and Marilyn J. Mason. *Facing Shame.* New York: W.W. Norton, 1986.

Friday, Nancy. *My Mother, Myself.* New York: Delacorte Press, 1977.

Friel, John and Linda Friel. *Adult Children: The Secrets of Dysfunctional Families.* Deerfield Beach, FL: Health Communcations, 1989.

Gilligan, Carol. *In a Different Voice.* Cambridge, MA: Harvard University Press, 1982.

Kaufman, Gershen. *Shame: The Power of Caring.* Cambridge, MA: Schenkman Books, 1985.

Leonard, Linda Schierse. *On the Way to the Wedding: Tranforming the Love Relationship.* Boston: Shambhala, 1987.

Leonard, Linda Schierse. *The Wounded Woman: Healing the Father-Daughter Relationship.* Boston: Shambhala, 1985.

Miller, Jean Baker. *Toward a New Psychology of Women.* Boston: Beacon Press, 1976.

Norwood, Robin. *Women Who Love Too Much.* New York: Simon and Schuster, 1985.

Page, Susan. *If I'm so Wonderful, Why Am I Still Single?* New York: Bantam Books, 1988.

Paul, Jordan and Margaret Paul. *Do I Have to Give Up Me to Be Loved by You?* Minneapolis: CompCare, 1983.

Payne, Karen. *Between Ourselves: Letter Between Mothers and Daughters.* Boston: Houghton Mifflin, 1983.

Scarf, Maggie. *Intimate Partners.* New York: Ballantine Books, 1988.

Wegscheider-Cruse, Sharon, and others. *Co-Dependency.* Deerfield Beach, FL: Health Communications, 1988.

Woititz, Janet. *Struggle for Intimacy.* Deerfield Beach, FL: Health Communications: 1985.

Woodman, Marion. *Addiction to Perfection.* Toronto: Inner City Books, 1982.

# About The
# Author

Karen Jenkins, MSW, a therapist in private practice in Orange, California, specializes in relationship issues and conducts groups for chronically single women and incest survivors. Jenkins was founder and director of the Co-Dependency Treatment Center, an association of mental health professionals who work with dysfunctional families. She is a technical consultant to film producers.

### Workshops And Lectures

Jenkins offers workshops and educational programs for chronically single women and therapists who treat them. For a schedule of events, or if you are interested in bringing a program to your area, please send your request with a self-addressed, stamped envelope to the address below.

The author welcomes any responses to *Chronically Single Women* but regrets that she is unable to answer individual letters.

Karen Jenkins, MSW
P.O. Box 5946
Orange, CA 92613-5946

# **M** ake a difference in your life with

### *Changes*
THE RECOVERY LIFESTYLE MAGAZINE

*CHANGES* is the only national magazine that keeps you informed about the latest and best in personal growth and recovery.

*CHANGES* offers thought-provoking feature stories and exciting special sections. Plus six enlightening features aimed at helping you heal and strengthen the important aspects of your life: Feelings, Relationships, Body, Working, Self-Esteem and Spirit.

Order *CHANGES* today and get our special offer to you: One year of *CHANGES* (six bi-monthly issues) for just $16.95. That's 44% off the regular subscription price, and a fraction of the annual newsstand price.

**Clip and mail this coupon to:**
**CHANGES Magazine, P.O. Box 609**
**Mount Morris, IL 61054-0609**

- - - - - - - - - - - - - - - - - - - - - - - - ✂ - - -

## YES! Enter my subscription to CHANGES for:

( ) one year for $16.95*
( ) two years for $33.00

Name: _____

Address: _____

City: _____ State: _____ Zip: _____

❏ Payment enclosed ❏ Please bill me          QCHC194

Charge my ❏VISA ❏MC #: _____

Exp ._____ Signature: _____

* Basic price: $30/yr. FL residents add 6% state sales tax. Canadian and foreign rates: $23.50 per year with order, US funds. GST included.